So You Think You Can Teach

So You Think You Can Teach

A Guide For New College Professors On How To Teach Adult Learners

DR. SHELTON J. GOODE

iUniverse, Inc.
Bloomington

SO YOU THINK YOU CAN TEACH
A GUIDE FOR NEW COLLEGE PROFESSORS ON HOW TO TEACH
ADULT LEARNERS

iUniverse books may be ordered through booksellers or by contacting:

iUniverse
1663 Liberty Drive
Bloomington, IN 47403
www.iuniverse.com
1-800-Authors (1-800-288-4677)

ISBN: 978-1-4620-1787-4 (sc)
ISBN: 978-1-4620-1789-8 (hc)
ISBN: 978-1-4620-1788-1 (ebk)

Printed in the United States of America

iUniverse rev. date: 11/03/2011

Contents

Dedication

I dedicate this book to thousands of working professional adult learners that I have taught during the past 15 years. They have helped me understand the power of education and inspired me with their thirst for knowledge. They exhibited uncommon courage as they pursued their educational goals, and they achieved exceptional results despite incredible challenges. Writing this book has reminded me how indebted I am to each and every student for placing their trust and confidence in me. I am humbled by the gift to teach and the opportunities I've had to grow and learn with my students as we strived to improve the human spirit and condition through education.

Acknowledgements

I am certain I would not have realized the goal of writing this book without the support from family, friends, and fellow colleagues. Appreciation is extended to the Troy University Atlanta campus faculty and staff whose constant support aided enormously in completing this book. A debt of gratitude is also owed to Dr. Steve Olson, and Dr. Felix Verdigets for their thorough and thoughtful critiques; and to Sandra Kinney and Dr. Charles Mitchell for the courage and generosity to share their insights with future college and university instructors. Every book starts with an idea and for that I am grateful to Pam Arnold, J.R. Hipple, Chuck McNair, who first encouraged me and then helped to shape the structure, direction, and content of the book. Lastly, to the editors who helped me decipher and organize over 300 pages of personal notes and archival documents. Each one of you deserve my heartfelt thanks and admiration.

Introduction

When I first started teaching at the college and university level in the 1990s, the world had become a very complex place, but the classroom had not. I walked into my Principles of Management classroom with my textbook, a cup of coffee, and absolutely no idea of how I was going to teach the course. I sat at a table at the front of the room and proceeded to utter nonsense for 50 minutes, and then scooted back to my office to grade a few papers and read the text. I was desperately trying to stay one chapter ahead of my students. I taught exactly as I had been taught by my professors at the liberal arts university in south Texas where I got my bachelor's degree.

Getting a teaching job back then was not especially difficult. I filled out the application, provided a copy of my transcript, showed up for a short interview with the department chair (and several hastily picked faculty members who happened to be available that day), and met for a few minutes with the dean. The next thing I knew, I received a letter informing me that I was hired as an adjunct instructor. I later found out that even though I had no college teaching experience and had received a C in algebra while an undergrad, I had impressed the department chair and the dean with my ability to connect with students. That was it! I was hired.

Things are very different today. The competition for jobs is infinitely tougher, and every person who wants to be a college instructor has to be able to effectively help the working professional adult learner achieve desired learning outcomes from day one. Unfortunately, I believe that most new college instructors still start out their teaching careers as I did 20 years ago. Not clueless, exactly . . . but not ready for prime time, either.

In 2003, a National Research Council report called for more instruction and training on how to effectively facilitate adult learning. Numerous publications have also sounded the alarm about the decline of student performance, creating a clear and present danger to our country's economic competitiveness. Specifically, between 2003 and 2008, the National Research Council found that 51 percent of college students did not complete degree requirements—and rates among women and minorities were significantly higher. This prompted some adult education experts to call for training and implementation of effective teaching approaches based on scientific research and methods.

The National Research Council specifically suggested designing training opportunities that are efficient and effective, that provide continuity, and that meet the needs of an increasingly diverse student population. Moreover, researcher Jeffrey Brainard suggested in a 2007 article in *The Chronicles of Higher Education* that s surprising new development, particularly at research universities, had eroded the quality of teaching at colleges and universities. Brainard argued that faculty resistance to diverting time from research—including student and postdoctoral research efforts—had contributed to a general lack of understanding of the components of effective teaching. This indictment against the quality of teaching at the college and university level is one of the driving forces that compelled me to write this book.

Traditional 18—to 22-year-old full-time undergraduate students account for only 16 percent of higher education enrollments. Yet scant attention is given to the larger group of students: "nontraditional," or working, professional adults struggling to balance jobs, families, and education. *This book aims to help individuals who are new to teaching at the college or university level better align their teaching methods to meet the needs of adult learners, thereby playing a critical role in increasing access to higher education.*

If you have recently been to a library for material on teaching, the array of topics and the number of specialized texts may have bewildered you. You'll find this book summarizes the best research of adult education experts. This book concentrates on the college classroom and university academic environment. People who must give briefings, communicate to large groups, or give speeches to various audiences may also find this book helpful.

This book will hopefully be relevant to new and prospective college instructors for several reasons. First, colleges and universities find themselves under immense pressure from the higher education accrediting agencies to prove students are actually learning. An example? The National Research Council reports that in the last five years, 35 to 40 schools have been placed on probation or received some level of sanction from an accrediting agency. This new level of accountability has created a mild panic in academia. One answer is for prospective and new college instructors to learn to adapt and use diverse teaching methods. Colleges increasingly look for instructors, in fact, who have had experience using new methods and current technologies to facilitate learning. This means more than putting together a course syllabus or effectively using PowerPoint during a lecture. New instructors must demonstrate the link between facilitation skills and students' learning and achievement.

This book will also give you a better understanding of what it takes to facilitate the learning of working professional adult students. If you are new to teaching at the college or university level, you should find this book particularly helpful—instead of improvising in the classroom as I did, you can approach your teaching more systematically. As a result, you and your students will benefit.

Finally, this book differs from other books that focus on technical and on-the-job training. Technical training normally includes a much higher proportion of the full range of theory and skills a student needs. For example, when technical students are tested, the instructor can be sure of what they know—tests offer the instructor "proof" students have mastered course material.

In academic instruction, the course usually has a more general range of possible skills, objectives, and content. Unlike technical instruction, the course often has no "cap," and students are encouraged to go beyond the minimum stated objectives. Instead of having technical instruction's "proof" of learning, the academic classroom often has only *samples* of learning as evidence. College instructors often must be satisfied with a sampling process when designing individual class periods and evaluating student achievement. This book helpfully focuses on academic—not technical—instruction at the university and college level.

What's here? Chapter 1 provides an overview of various teaching methods. Chapter 2 discusses how to manage classroom diversity by valuing individual student differences. Chapters 3 through 6 focus on valuable teaching methods: lecture, case study, teaching interview, and experiential. Chapter 7 provides guidance on how to effectively use questions to facilitate adult learning. Chapter 8 offers techniques on giving feedback to adult students. Chapter 9 discusses the virtual classroom and distance learning. And Chapter 10 shows how to reinforce student confidence.

In the last 20 years, I have watched the vision and mission of colleges and universities undergo a significant transition. This transformation accelerated in the 1990s, when corporations and private businesses started underwriting for-profit colleges and universities all over the country. Teaching in the 1990s grew exciting, with new autonomy and freedom. If you needed a new course, you simply wrote one. If you needed a new program, you created one. Didn't have a process to fit your purpose? You developed one.

Today, teaching requires even more creativity and invention. The diversity of adult learners, the popularity and growing acceptance of virtual teaching, and the complexity of educational technology has created a learning environment in which college instructors must possess a greater depth and breadth of competencies than ever before.

Extensive as this book may appear, it cannot provide you with the final stages of the process: teaching and being judged on your teaching skills. Even experienced college professors profit from constructive feedback from other professors and faculty members regarding lesson preparation and presentation. Turn to your fellow faculty members to learn from their varied experiences. The more we share what works—and what does not—the more we will help our students learn, grow, and develop.

Chapter 1

Survey of Teaching Methods

Introduction

The way you teach is as important as what you teach.

Good objectives will be wasted if the teaching method is poor, but even the best methods will have little or no value if courses lack objectives. This chapter and several that follow discuss various ways to deliver instruction—the teaching methods.

As illustrated by Figure 1, adult learning begins with a student who has a desire for new knowledge or a need for new experience. The learning process is facilitated by an instructor who has the required knowledge and experience to help the student achieve his or her outcomes. The instructor and student act as partners in the educational journey, with a common understanding of the objectives and with active dual participation in the learning process. Learning may involve various teaching methods, criterion-based evaluations of student performance—and candid, frequent, ongoing feedback.

After determining the lesson objective, choose a method of instruction based on the student's abilities as a learner. Remember that adult students learn best by doing, discussing, listening, observing, and participating. The instructor's role? Selecting a teaching method that will result in the most meaningful learning experience.

Keys to Adult Learning

This chapter surveys a number of teaching methods. Although descriptions are short, there should be enough detail to identify methods that deserve further study. Four teaching methods (lecture, teaching interview, case study, and experiential) are described in considerable detail in subsequent chapters. They merit closer discussion because of their specific applicability to college or university classroom instruction.

For the sake of clarity, the individual methods described in this chapter have been grouped into five broad categories—presentation methods, demonstration-performance methods, self-paced methods, discussion methods, and application methods. Remember that no one particular method is suitable for every teaching situation.

Presentation Methods

Presentation learning methods provide situations in which the skill or material to be learned is in some way presented to, or demonstrated for, the learner. Some presentation methods require little, if any, activity from students other than their attention. Others demand considerable student participation. What distinguishes these methods from other categories? Students begin the learning experience here with little or no previous exposure to the material or skills to be learned.

Teaching Lecture—The lecture is a formal or informal presentation of information, concepts, or principles. The formal lecture is usually presented to large groups of people (more than 50), with no active participation by the students. The learning experience is essentially passive. The informal lecture targets smaller groups and students participate by responding to questions.

Briefing—The briefing, a formal or informal presentation in which a variety of significant facts are presented as concisely as possible, is not strictly a teaching method but is sometimes used in school situations. Briefings rarely cover material beyond the knowledge level of the audience, and are almost always accompanied by visual representation of the material as charts, graphs, or PowerPoint slides.

Guest Lecture—A guest instructor brings variety to the class and provides information in an area where the primary instructor may not be an expert.

Dialogue—Dialogue occurs with the interaction between two or more persons, one of whom may be an instructor. Sharply opposing points of view may be presented. The dialogue is often highly structured toward preplanned learning objectives, and it may take the form of questions and answers.

Teaching Interview—In a teaching interview, the instructor questions a visiting expert and follows a highly structured plan that leads to educational objectives. The advantage of the teaching interview over the guest lecture? The instructor controls the expert's presentation. Students can interact with the subject matter expert during a question-and-answer period that follows the interview.

Panel—A panel is a structured or unstructured discussion involving two or more experts, generally facilitated by the instructor. A panel can be presented in a variety of ways, such as constructive arguments followed by debate, response to questions from the instructor or students, a preplanned agenda, a fixed or a random order of speakers, or free discussion.

Skits, Mini-Plays, and Other Dramatizations—These methods often effectively introduce variety into instruction and learning. A subdivision of dramatization is role-playing by a college instructor to point out good or bad examples. (Role-playing by the college instructor differs from role-playing by students, a simulation method.)

Demonstration-Performance Methods

The demonstration-performance is the presentation or portrayal of a sequence of events to show a procedure, technique, or operation. It frequently combines oral explanation with the operation or handling of systems, equipment, or material. This method commonly supports small-group learning in a classroom or laboratory. It requires significant instructor guidance and feedback.

Coaching—Coaching is a formal, student-centered activity generally involving a college instructor and learner in a one-on-one relationship. Coaching can help students prepare for experiential activities, help them get ahead, or help learners with special needs. Whether used for an individual or for small groups, coaching requires significant student involvement and instructor feedback.

A videotape of student performance is an excellent coaching aid when supplemented by a college instructor's analysis and critique . . . and is particularly effective at improving the teaching and facilitation skills of new college instructors.

Self-Paced Methods

Self-paced instruction allows students to learn at their own speed under the guidance of a college instructor. Examples include programmed instruction, modular instruction, and computer-assisted instruction.

Programmed Instruction provides a carefully planned sequence of small units of instruction, requiring the learner to respond to cues and receive immediate feedback. Various media can be used.

Modular Instruction consists of prepackaged units of instruction that typically contain a clear statement of objectives and all necessary resources to help the learner achieve desired outcomes. A module can be a complete unit or part of a course.

Computer-Assisted Instruction uses a computer as the vehicle for interaction between the learner and the course of instruction. It may include support tools, such as video vignettes.

Discussion Methods

Enhanced learning may be the reward when students deal with material as a team. There are several types of group discussion, most requiring previous preparation by students.

The Socratic Method can be used to emphasize a point, stimulate thinking, keep students alert, check understanding, review material, and seek clarification. It may resemble a guided discussion, but the goal is often to obtain specific answers to specific questions (reiteration) and not to stimulate discussion. The Socratic method can expose inconsistencies in students' logic, sharpening their thinking skills. Law professors often use the method for "interrogating" specific students, using a series of questions as they might be used in a courtroom.

Appreciative Inquiry—students asking questions—is often used in combination with the lecture, panel discussion, or teaching interview. It may also be used by itself, either one-to-one in tutoring or coaching, or as part of small or large groups. Students control this method, although the responder, if skilled, can also control the session. Student questions are a measure of how well they understand a particular matter; they need a certain degree of knowledge to ask the right questions.

Non-Guided Discussion is a teaching method that is controlled by students. The college instructor normally plays a limited or passive role. One example? The peer-controlled seminar, in which a group of highly qualified students (doctoral or law school) meet periodically to exchange ideas. Another is the research seminar, in which the instructor allows qualified students to lead the discussion, with his or her supervision. In many professional and post-graduate programs, it's not unusual to find a student acting as a peer facilitator and leading discussions or conducting seminars. In this process, the instructor provides a statement of the educational objectives and a discussion guide . . . and also requires some tangible evidence of the discussion results.

Guided Discussion Method is an instructor-led, interactive process of sharing information and experiences. The difference between non-guided and guided discussion? The instructor's active involvement in asking questions and summarizing concepts and principles. The instructor interacts with the group as a whole through questions, but does not dominate the discussion. Students learn about a subject by actively sharing ideas, knowledge, and opinions.

Application Methods

Application methods give students opportunities to apply what they've learned to practical situations. Some application methods ask students to relate learned material to new experiences and recognize how the material applies—that is, to transfer concepts to new situations. In other application methods, students apply previously learned material to new situations to make decisions or solve problems.

Individual Projects usually take place outside the classroom and require students to interact with data or people to achieve learning outcomes. Instructors provide feedback periodically, or as needed. Examples of individual projects include research papers, theses, and dissertations.

Field Trips are out-of-classroom experiences in which students interact with persons, locations, and materials to achieve learning objectives. Students learn from experiences in real-world settings.

Case Studies are learning experiences in which students study a real-life situation in order to learn. Realistic cases help students develop new insights into solving specific real-world problems. Students also acquire knowledge of practical concepts and principles used in problem solving. Case study design helps students reach the higher levels of learning—application, analysis, synthesis, and evaluation. The complexity of a case, the difficulties of the learning objectives, and how the case is conducted influence whether this method effectively helps students learn.

In **Experiential Learning**, students participate in structured learning activities that focus on a specific learning objective. Ideally, the activities have a direct real-world relevancy. The following activities typify experiential learning:

- **Simulations** are low-risk educational experiences that substitute for a real-life situation. Although they require a lot of classroom time, simulations prove especially effective as capstone methods following a program or a course. Elaborate simulations may require special equipment, larger classrooms, different classroom configurations, and specially trained staff. Simulations often use hardware or technology comparable to what's found in a typical workplace. For example, students may train on equipment that resembles, to some degree, the equipment they'll use on a job. A good example is a flight simulator, which has characteristics of an airplane cockpit. Simulators teach effectively when the actual equipment is too costly or otherwise impractical.

- **Role-Playing.** Students project themselves into simulated interpersonal situations and act out the parts of persons and situations assigned by the instructor. Role-playing proves particularly effective for practicing interpersonal skills such as counseling, interviewing, and teaching.

- **E-Mail In-Box Exercises** are used in random order to simulate a series of decisions a student might actually encounter. Students are confronted with a time-sensitive situation, limited information, and a list of action items that might be found in a typical e-mail in-box. After sorting out priorities, students dispose of e-mails by replying, delegating, setting up meetings, or delaying action.

- **Strategic Exercises** include varying degrees of competition between teams of students. Many complex and sophisticated exercises require a computer to support the simulation. Strategic experiential exercises include: (1) elements of conflict; (2) rules of engagement; (3) controlled moves; (4) rules of exercise termination; and (5) adaptable content based on the specific lesson objective. Strategic experiential exercises provide the new college instructor an excellent way to motivate students, to get them to interact, and to evaluate them in a non-threatening manner.

Summary

This chapter provided a brief overview of teaching methods grouped under the broad categories of presentation, demonstration-performance, self-paced, discussion, and application. There's just enough detail for you to determine whether further study might be worthwhile. Four of these methods will be detailed in chapters that follow.

Chapter 2

Managing Classroom Diversity

<u>No man is an island</u>. The English poet John Donne wrote those words nearly four centuries ago. They were true then, and they are true now.

Still, I have rarely felt more like an island—and an island in a forgotten sea—than in one certain situation I faced as an instructor for my graduate course in ethics at Troy University.

Troy University educates a high number of adult learners who are working professionals. Many other universities also seek out these non-traditional students these days, and for this reason college and university classrooms have become more diverse. Students may range from bright-eyed recent undergraduates who have Ph.D.s dancing in their eyes, to silver-haired working professionals who have returned to school to learn new skills for new jobs.

The diversity in my ethics class initially caught me off guard. I recognized the visible differences—students were white, black, and brown. Men and women. Buttoned-down and tattooed. But here was the big surprise—I had students from four different <u>generations</u> in one classroom! One of my students hadn't darkened the door of a classroom in 40 years!

There I was with more than 20 years of teaching experience and a solid mastery of most educational methods, facing the instructional equivalent of climbing Mt. Everest. One generation of students had always learned by formal lecture—stories, context, and background, followed by a closed-book multiple-choice test. One generation had grown up at a time when instruction was more personal, peppered with humor and anecdotes and the "why" to go along with the history. One generation just wanted to quickly get the bottom line—"Tell me what to learn, let me go learn it, don't keep me cooped up here." And one generation didn't really even want to be in a classroom at all—"Just post the information on Blackboard, Facebook or in whatever and allow me to get the assignments and material at my convenience."

Along with the mixture of students and their different learning styles and the familiar aspects of diversity—ethnicity, religion, gender, capability, etc.—came tremendous academic pressure. I taught a graduate course. Students who made two C grades could be put on probation for a year. Every good instructor wants students to do well . . . not have dreams stunted or deferred by probation.

All in all, I can remember times that semester when I felt like the proverbial man up the creek in a canoe without a paddle.

The solution? It was easy. It was also very hard.

I taught differently. I adapted my teaching style and methods to match the diversity of my students. This ensured that the course lesson reached each of the generational learning styles in the class <u>on their own terms</u>.

It was, of course, a ton of work. It meant PowerPoint slides . . . but also printed handouts. It meant lectures . . . and electronic postings on Facebook. It meant classic whiteboards . . . and scanned PDFs. It meant raise-your-hand-if-you-know-the-answer . . . and huge amounts of information on flash drives that went home with students. In short, it meant mixing in old-fashioned teaching methods with ultra-new methods. It meant I worked harder to help that class succeed than I did for any other class I'd ever had.

It also meant I personally learned a tremendous amount. I learned to teach differently. I learned to value diverse learning styles just as much as diversity of race, gender or age. I learned the value of teamwork—to depend more on colleagues than ever before. I learned how to manage new technologies, social media applications, and the Blackboard learning management system. And I learned to humbly seek out good advice from my students with diverse backgrounds.

In short, when it came to adapting <u>my own style as an instructor</u>— the great lesson this class taught me—this class underscored the importance of valuing the differences of my students and creating an inclusive learning environment. By working together with my students, we built a bridge between my teaching style and their learning needs. Because of this effort, my students were able to have their best shot at achieving their educational goals.

The poet had it right. <u>No man is an island</u>.

But if John Donne were alive today, he'd send out tweets with links to the full text of his poems. AND he'd provide handouts to the students who learned best from old-fashioned paper and ink. And he'd talk a lot with his colleagues about the best ways to put little islands of knowledge inside the heads of students with different backgrounds and learning styles. In short, he'd adapt his teaching methods to address the needs of his diverse students.

Now, that's instruction.

Introduction

As more students attend postsecondary institutions, and as our society experiences significant demographic changes, instructors feel the impact of ever-greater diversity in their classrooms. Diversity shows up in the classroom in many ways—gender, race, ethnicity, language, sexual orientation, age, religion, special physical needs, special mental needs, and learning ability. Diversity also includes nontraditional learners (such as part-time students or students with children) and at-risk learners (such as students facing financial challenges, students with weak language skills, and students with limited college preparation). Managing classroom dynamics that arise from diversity poses important challenges to every instructor . . . but especially new ones.

Add to this mix Generation X and Millennial learners—students born after 1985 who use technology as a normal part of their everyday lives. Generation Xers and Millenials learn differently from previous generations. They have a faster response time to questions and have an enhanced ability to piece together information from multiple sources and visual images. They use inductive discovery (the scientific method). We hear those from Generation X and Millennial generations often described as being digitally literate, technology-connected, multitaskers, experiential learners, prolific social communicators, team players, and demanding of structure. They expect parameters, rules, and procedures. They're visual and kinesthetic, and concerned with things that matter.

Effectively managing classroom diversity represents a potentially powerful and beneficial learning experience not only for the student, but for the instructor. Unattended, diversity issues can undermine the foundation of the learning environment and erode student confidence in the instructor.

Diversity 101: A Primer for the New College Instructor

College and university instructors increasingly fret over how to manage diversity issues so that all students feel included, not marginalized. Creating a safe and comfortable learning environment requires that all students feel they have a place and a voice in the classroom, that they can express themselves without fear, that they feel their experiences are valid, and that they know their contributions are valued.

A main goal of education is to learn *about* others and *from* others. But there's a formidable barrier to mutual understanding and tolerance—ethnocentrism, the belief that a certain culture's way of thinking is the only correct way. Ironically, ethnocentrism remains a problem even in light of our growing emphasis on multiculturalism. The problem includes resistance to racial, ethnic, cultural, geographic, sexual, and religious differences. It can have devastating effects on the classroom environment.

We all want to ensure that classrooms offer a safe space for students to speak. We once believed that if we as college instructors and role models treated each of our students with respect by valuing their differences, they in turn would treat others the same way. Unfortunately, we live in a world where difference is too often feared, ridiculed, or disparaged. What can college instructors do to manage diversity and to create an inclusive classroom? What measures can we take to effectively help our students value differences and to foster an atmosphere of openness? How can we encourage understanding and respect, not only in our classrooms but among all members of the college community and beyond?

The challenge can be met. We must ensure our students feel safe and, at a deeper level, we must raise their awareness of diversity. To achieve this, we first must understand the barriers to diversity and inclusion, and devise strategies to overcome them.

Barriers to Diversity and Inclusion in the Classroom

The following situations can stifle learning in a classroom:

- An instructor is unaware of how cultural differences regarding education influence student participation.

- An instructor allows certain students (who happen to be the same race, ethnicity, or gender as the instructor) to dominate class discussions, effectively silencing other students.

- A student makes a sexist remark, alienating other students.

- A student wears a T-shirt that bears a homophobic remark or diagram, alienating and negatively impacting gay, lesbian, bisexual, or transgendered students.

- An instructor only directs questions to or answers questions from students of one gender (whether male or female).

- An instructor allows students to denounce or ridicule the gender, sexual preference, race, ethnicity, or religion of other students.

In these examples, both instructor and students prove guilty of behaviors that make some students feel they are not valued and respected. It hardly matters whether the instructor directly engages in these behaviors or allows them to go unchecked. The results are equally damaging. Such situations create tension in the classroom. They also set a tone that can cause students to disengage from the learning process.

Let's look more closely at two of these examples, and discuss strategies to effectively manage them.

Take the first example: *The instructor is unaware of how cultural differences regarding education influence student participation.* This situation concerns culture and learning in general, but more specifically cultural *interpretations* of what constitutes class participation. Most instructors encourage students to participate in class by expressing their opinions, answering questions, and responding to other students. Some students, however, come from cultures that discourage students from verbal or active participation. Students in these cultures expect to passively receive the instructor's knowledge, as if poured into them like water. A college instructor with little awareness of cultural differences and their impact on learning might perceive such students as disinterested or lazy.

It is especially important for a new instructor to be a keen observer of student behavior and interaction. Look for signs of discomfort. Discretely ask questions to discover the cause of a student's silence. Doing so will bring you closer to finding the real reasons behind a student's behavior and will show the student you value and respect him or her. This builds rapport and increases the student's confidence. This may also open a dialogue, and an opportunity to find other ways to get the student more involved in class activities and discussions.

The second example: *The instructor allows certain students to dominate class discussions, thus silencing the other students.* This can be illustrated by a case in which the women in the class have to struggle to make their comments heard because the male instructor never curtails dominant male speakers. The instructor either consciously or unconsciously fails the female students by not carefully facilitating classroom discussions. Regardless of the instructor's intent, the women in the classroom feel alienated, frustrated, and shut out of the learning process. This type of marginalization especially damages newer students, who tend to be less sure of their worth in a classroom setting.

Understanding Individual Differences

Students will arrive with different personalities, motivations, past achievements, and abilities. We can't change their pasts or personalities. We can, however, provide an environment that motivates them, and we can create opportunities to help them make the best use of their abilities.

Differences in Motivation—Motivation is the difference of most concern to college instructors. Why? Motivated students learn more effectively, and unmotivated students are more likely to be a disturbing influence on others. Motivation may be as diverse as your students. Some students will strive for excellence in all aspects of a course. Some will be motivated only when external rewards (such as grades or the opportunity to be a distinguished graduate) are at stake. Still others will exert only enough effort to meet the minimum criteria for passing.

Try these simple steps for motivating students:

- Offer verbal praise.

- Put personal notes on tests and other written assignments.

- Motivate with grades or similar performance rewards.

- Give positive reinforcement at the appropriate time.

- Use familiar examples.

- Build on previous instruction.

- Win the support of classroom leaders.

- Use computers, simulations, and experiential exercises.

Differences in Ability—The testing movement during the 1920s revealed a wide range of student intelligence quotients in typical public school classrooms. Studies indicated that the brightest students could move at a more rapid pace than less able students. The findings raised questions about accepted teaching methods and indicated that certain materials, texts, and topics might be inappropriate for many students. Researchers concluded that any attempt to teach students in a group would likely miss the mark for some fellow students.

A number of college instructors attempted to address the issue with individualized instruction methods, allowing students to work on tasks appropriate to their particular abilities. For example, instructors chose the goals of instruction, learning materials, subject matter, and teaching method especially for a particular student or a small group of students with common characteristics. In some cases, students were placed in a special seminar, with the academic program tailored to their needs. To the extent possible, they moved at their own pace.

Differences in Learning Style—Students learn in many ways. They perceive, think, and solve problems differently, meaning they have different cognitive learning styles.

Many colleges and universities have used students' cognitive learning styles as a basis for placing students in certain courses. These schools report that students' grades improved and their anxiety dropped.

Understanding Group Differences

The results of research on group differences are often of limited use to educators because of the controversy they generate or because one study conflicts with another. Nonetheless, useful, if tentative, conclusions have been drawn in some areas of study, with implications for classroom college instructors. An example? Much research has investigated gender differences in the classroom. Although differences in verbal, visual-spatial, and mathematical ability do exist between the sexes, the cumulative research on ability and actual school achievement does not offer sufficient evidence for treating adults differently based purely on their gender. More importantly, research findings suggest that college instructors should not hold different expectations of cognitive performance for the sexes.

Recognizing Your Personal Biases

Oversimplified, rigid beliefs about categories of people—biases—tend to be invalid. If you believe that all female students are poor students or all Asian students are good in math, then you overgeneralize. You form stereotypes. Moreover, if you believe males outperform females on visual-spatial tasks, or that females outdo males in tasks that involve understanding and producing language, you may be shortchanging your relationships with students.

Examine your ideas of stereotypes. Decide how these might be influencing your behavior in the classroom. You'll be a better teacher, and you'll have better classrooms by eliminating unsupported beliefs and the influence they have on your behavior.

Most students do not want to be treated differently based on age, sex, race, or background. Avoid actions that offend them or cause them to lose interest in your class. Students deserve to be respected for who and what they are, just as we all do. The following suggestions are by no means comprehensive, but offer a starting point for more dialogue and ideas.

- Initiate and attend regular discussion groups for instructors to address practical diversity issues, such as how our perceptions, values, and beliefs influence and create a frame in the classroom.

- Monitor conflicts in the classroom. Pay attention to what led to each particular incident. How did you deal with it? What was the outcome? How did it affect the students and learning environment?

- Create a safe place for students to discuss diversity issues.

- Train your fellow instructors using videotaped vignettes of situations. Follow by brainstorming solutions to problems.

How to avoid bias? Look in the mirror. Start with a self-reflective journey that explores and defines your own biases. You might participate in a campus diversity working group or workshop—if one does not exist, then start one. Experiential workshops and exercises can emphasize the development of skills and behaviors you'll need to facilitate student growth and understanding, rather than silence and alienation. A clear and positive sense of your own identity can lead to an appreciation of similarities and differences between you and your students. Such differences will seem less threatening, and the increased awareness will enhance your classroom effectiveness. The payoff for your students? A more positive environment and a richer learning experience.

Creating an Inclusive Classroom Environment

My daughter's undergraduate experience has shaped my own approach as an instructor. In her particular case, it was a case of learning things backward—what an instructor should not do, rather than do.

During her political science studies at a university notable for its international diversity and age diversity, my daughter had two instructors who could have used some instruction in how to adapt their teaching methods and styles to match the learning styles of their students.

One instructor was a native of Nigeria who came to class with a pedantic, locked-down regimen of lectures, assignments, and tests. His preferred teaching method did not accommodate in the least the unfortunate members of his classes who were from other nationalities themselves or who did not have the same resources to meet the instructor's course demands outside the classroom as their American counterparts. This instructor never requested feedback or allowed healthy interaction in classes. His terse, autocratic style and dogmatic approach created tensions and completely turned some students off from his course . . . and perhaps even their career plans. He offered my daughter and me an example of how to ineffectively transfer knowledge . . . and damage an innocent classroom's passion for learning.

The second instructor was a white male from a rural Georgia background. He often spiced his lectures with colloquialisms and idioms that utterly baffled his international students, some of whom were still doing their best to learn English completely. When the instructor mentioned in one lecture that "you guys are learning this stuff slower than molasses in winter," my daughter watched as her international classmates turned to her with helpless panic in their eyes. Needless to say, she spent a lot of her time that semester as an unofficial interpreter, repeatedly communicating the meaning of the instructor's riddles to classmates.

As is plain in these examples, instructors must recognize, value, and respond to the diversity of the students in their classrooms. Instructors must create an inclusive learning environment by adapting their teaching methods to students of a 21st-century setting—students who almost surely will vary in age, ethnicity, technical prowess, national origin, and even the ability to speak English fluently. Valuing the diversity of students and creating an inclusive learning environment for them is the best way to set the stage for success. That's success for each student . . . and success for your own future as an instructor.

Your goal for creating an inclusive classroom should be to help your students learn, regardless of who they are or where they come from. Making all students feel valued, respected, and productive involves three tactics: managing your presence in the classroom, being creative, and using a variety of teaching methods.

Manage Your Classroom Presence—If there is little discussion, ask yourself if you're showing enough concern for your students. Rather than allowing one student to dominate the conversation, encourage all students to participate. If you make it a practice to call on non-volunteers, everyone soon gets the idea they are responsible for participating.

Be tactful in drawing out quiet students. The least effective approach is surprising the student with, **"What do you think about this point, John?"** Often, simple eye contact will encourage a response, rather than direct by-name confrontation. Reasons for silence among students vary. A student may not be prepared. A student may feel ill at ease in a group. A student may simply be thoughtful (or thoughtless). When a topic is new, challenging, or complex, some students need more time than others to get into it.

As you consider individual differences, don't embarrass your students. If someone has been inattentive, choose a question you think that person can easily answer. Or start with a recall question. Do not embarrass an inattentive student with a difficult question. Make all your students feel that they have a stake in the success of the class.

Be accepting of your students, and genuinely seek out their responses. Your body language, facial expressions, mannerisms, and tone of voice all play a part in encouraging or discouraging student participation.

Be careful not to cut someone off too quickly. Even though an answer may sound inappropriate, give the student a chance to explain. Part of the answer may turn out to be correct. Even if it's not, you may learn valuable clues to student difficulties and a basis for reteaching. Your criticism at this point might cause the student to withdraw completely.

If students ask impertinent or off-subject questions, tactfully defer the answer until later. Sometimes, forgetting a question ever came up is a good idea.

Use Creativity—We sometimes hear critics say college instructors lack creativity, that our dull presentations are more briefings than true lectures. Students accuse college instructors of being stiff, expressionless, and unable to communicate effectively with a diverse audience. Consequently, students often feel forced to memorize large amounts of basic information. We must avoid letting modern technology turn our well-intended teaching efforts into PowerPoint bores or "talking head" presentations.

Be constantly aware of the barriers to creativity. Anything that inhibits the ability to be free, natural, and spontaneous limits the opportunity for creative ideas.

Researchers have identified four broad categories of barriers to creativity in teaching: inertia, fear, prejudice, and habit. Inertia causes many of us to continue doing precisely what we've always done, unless challenged to change. College instructors who fear being different avoid attention by keeping to the status quo, leaving things as they are. Prejudiced instructors reject new approaches and methods because they automatically dismiss anything new without trying it. Habit is a very real problem, leading to courses taught the same way, time after time, simply because "that's how it's always been done."

How do you fight to keep an inclusive learning environment? Ensure that classrooms, labs, and field work are accessible to individuals with a wide range of physical abilities. Make sure equipment and activities minimize sustained physical effort, so that people with different physical abilities can still participate. (Simple things matter: How often have you taken into consideration that some of your students may be left-handed?) Also, assure the safety of all students and minimize the need for unnecessary physical travel by making materials available at hand, or by allowing them to be submitted electronically.

Be a creative facilitator of adult learning. Know when to use time-tested methods. Know when to strike out boldly in new directions.

Use a Variety of Teaching Methods—After deciding exactly what to teach, determine how best to teach it and what instructional method to use. A method is a broad approach to instruction (i.e., lecture, guided, case study). A technique is a specific, concrete skill or procedure used in implementing a method—for example, the technique of using a computer or using a Harvard Business Case as support material.

Choose a teaching method best suited to students' needs. In your selection, consider the ways people learn—by doing, discussing, listening, observing, and participating. Select the instructional method most effective for guiding students toward the learning outcomes you desire.

Keep in mind that *no one method is sufficiently flexible to meet the needs of all students in every situation.* If, for example, you want students to gain skill in performing a certain task, a natural activity would be practice at performing the task. If the desired outcome is knowledge, students should observe, listen, and read to relate what they learn to their own experiences. If students must learn to apply a principle, the instructor could be effective by asking them to solve problems or perform tasks that require an application of that principle. The instructional approach you choose for one learning outcome may differ from the approaches you select for other outcomes in the same lesson.

What's the final word here? Master a variety of teaching methods, and make sure the methods you choose are clear and appropriate for students with a wide range of abilities, backgrounds, and experiences.

You'll be a better teacher. And you'll have better students.

<u>Summary</u>

You have a responsibility to your students to raise your awareness about the implications of increased diversity in your classrooms. Be a role model. Embrace students' differences, creating an atmosphere of mutual respect. By taking a proactive approach to diversity, you can support all the students in your classroom and move away from the ethnocentric attitudes that have sometimes dominated our educational institutions. By recognizing that life circumstances are vastly different, you can begin to draw rich lessons from the diversity of your students. You can enrich and enhance the learning experience not only for your students, but for yourself.

Make it your personal mission to penetrate areas of resistance and silence. Raise awareness about different identities and communities.

Encourage mutual understanding and respect. As an educator, you can help your students value differences by developing an understanding of the larger contextual issues of gender, race, culture, and ethnicity.

Do what you can to overcome biases against groups based on sex, age, race, or background. Those are tough problems for any instructor. A good start is eliminating stereotypes. Also, apply caution in interpreting group averages, and recognize that you do have limitations in coping with student differences.

Students will vary in their motivation and ability. Some will be fully motivated by the need to achieve. Others may be motivated by a fear of failure. Affiliation, power, and recognition also motivate students. Frustration can too, but frustrated behavior often trends in a socially undesirable direction.

Diversity in the classroom presents challenges, yet it also opens many opportunities for instructors. You can manage diversity and create an inclusive learning environment by (1) encouraging the exchange of diverse ideas; (2) fostering an open atmosphere for provocative and intelligent discussion; (3) facilitating critical and thoughtful discussions; (4) defusing potential conflicts; and (5) providing the best learning environment for each and every student.

Of course, all this is easy to say, but hard to do. You may at times feel like you're changing a tire on a speeding car. Just remember that success is out there—many of us have met with great success and personal satisfaction as we worked with our classrooms of diverse learners.

Chapter 3

Lecture Method

The French playwright Marcel Archard wryly summed up the feeling that students sometimes hold for the classroom lecture.

"When I give a lecture," Archard said, "I accept that people look at their watches. But what I do not tolerate is when they look at it and raise it to their ear to find out if it stopped."

Ouch. I feel a twinge of guilt . . . and you may too, if you've ever had one of those days when despite your best effort, a lecture missed the mark.

Still, there's a fundamental reason instruction has depended on the lecture as a teaching method for hundreds of years.

Lectures <u>work</u>.

A lecture, prepared well, delivered well, and tested well, is a primary means of passing valuable information from one mind to another—or to many others. Experience may indeed be the best teacher, but the sharing of experience by a knowledgeable person with an audience places a close second.

This chapter aims to help you be a better lecturer. There's much good information here. And remember—you may not ever be able to stop a student or two from watching the clock . . . but a good lecture has a way of making time fly, along with useful information.

Introduction

Traditionally, lecturing has been the most popular teaching method at colleges and universities. College instructors lecture to teach large groups of students in auditoriums, or to explain a subject or a process briefly to smaller groups before proceeding with some other activity or method.

Types of Lectures

A teaching lecture is a presentation of information, concepts, or principles by a single instructor to a group of students. We recognize several types of lectures—formal, informal, briefing, and speech.

Formal Lecture—Normally, a formal lecture is a one-way interaction with an instructor or an expert conveying information to students. Student participation is limited. Impersonal and usually given to a large group, the formal lecture can seem very structured and rehearsed. Still, it can be delivered in a natural and conversational delivery style, without overuse of notes.

Informal Lecture—The audience for an informal lecture is usually smaller, and there may be considerable student participation and interaction, usually in the form of questions and discussion. Stylistically, the delivery style is conversational. Informal lecturers often address students by name.

Briefing—A briefing informs rather than teaches. With its format or structure often fixed, the briefing may cover different subjects arranged topically in the same order, day after day. A briefing often forms the basis for a decision or action. New college instructors often present very formal briefings, while more seasoned and experienced instructors may infuse briefings with their personalities or humorous material. The instructor usually does not worry about learning techniques such as interim summaries, repetition, and extended conclusions. Interaction between the instructor and students usually ends with questions about the material. As a college or university instructor, you may occasionally present briefings. It's best, though, to avoid a teaching presentation style that relies too heavily on them.

Speech—A speech generally has one of three basic purposes—to inform, persuade, or entertain. The *informative speech* concerns a specific topic but doesn't involve a sustained effort to teach. A talk or presentation at new-student orientation is a good example. The *persuasive speech* means to move an audience to belief or action on some topic, product, or issue. Military recruiters talking to a high school graduating class or a dissertation defense summation are two examples of a persuasive speech. The *entertaining speech* gives enjoyment to an audience, often through humor and vivid language. A speech at an annual faculty award dinner illustrates the form.

Instructors sometimes want to accomplish all three basic purposes of speech-making. We attempt to <u>inform</u> students on a given subject. When we try to <u>influence</u> students to modify their behavior, we become persuaders. And it may be advantageous at times to gain attention by <u>entertaining</u>. We can skillfully mix these purposes to facilitate student learning.

Advantages and Disadvantages of the Lecture Method

In some college classrooms, the method of instruction is set in stone, leaving you with a limited role in deciding how to present material. In other cases, it may be your job to choose the method to use for a lesson or a series of lessons. Select the appropriate method only after you write down your learning objectives and complete your initial research on the subject. Also be aware of the advantages and disadvantages of the lecture method.

Advantages—The lecture is one of the most efficient ways to present many facts or ideas in a short time to a large audience. Material that has been logically organized can be presented concisely in rapid sequence. Because of its advantages, a majority of college and university instructors use the lecture method at least part of the time.

- The lecture is particularly suitable for introducing a subject. To ensure all students have the necessary background to learn a subject, we can present basic information to students with diverse backgrounds and create a common understanding. A brief introductory lecture can give direction and purpose to a demonstration, or prepare students for a discussion.

- Not only is the lecture a convenient method for instructing large groups, it also can be the most efficient method to use in settings with a high student-to-faculty ratio.

- The lecture often supplements material from other sources or information difficult to obtain in other ways. If students do not have time for research or if they do not have access to reference material, a good lecture fills the gap. In subject areas where information is available from a variety of sources, such as textbooks or journals, the lecture allows you to summarize and emphasize pertinent material. Reports, current research, and information that changes frequently may not be easy to find in written form. The lecture can effectively give students the most current information.

- The lecture allows a large number of students to receive information from a person who can speak from actual experience or a scholar who has carefully analyzed the results of research. These experts can have great credibility with students. The energy and enthusiasm of a person with actual experience in a field can motivate students tremendously.

Disadvantages

- Speech skills, cooperative group thinking, and motor skills are difficult to teach with the lecture method. (Students best develop such skills through practice.) Because it allows for little or no student participation, the formal lecture may be unsuitable for certain lessons involving concepts and principles.

- The formal lecture alone is generally not appropriate for presenting material above the comprehension level of learning.

- The lecture does not provide instructors with an opportunity to gauge student progress before an exam. In a single lecture period, the instructor may unwittingly present more information than students can absorb. As a result, the instructor may not know what students have really learned.

- Learning is an active process, but the lecture method tends to foster passiveness among students and a dependence on the instructor. Because the lecture does not provide an opportunity for student participation, some students willingly allow the instructor to do all the work.

- Instructors may have to spend a significant amount of time preparing for lectures. A greater burden for the total lesson rests here on the instructor than in case studies, group discussion, or other methods.

- Many instructors find it difficult to hold the attention of their students when they lecture for an entire class period. To use the lecture method effectively, you obviously need considerable speaking skills.

The first three disadvantages of the lecture, which include difficulty in achieving certain types of learning and ineffectiveness of assessing student learning, are inherent to the method. The fourth disadvantage, student passivity, can be alleviated with an effective informal lecture. The final two disadvantages provide the focus for the remainder of this chapter.

Planning the Lecture

The first order of business? Know your audience. That is, analyze your class. Because students tend to be passive when hearing a lecture, your analysis of students will greatly influence how you plan your instruction.

Organize the information you already have about the students. What do you know about their age, gender, course prerequisites, and experience? Understanding these variables can help you relate to your audience. Give special attention to ways of emphasizing your similarities and reducing differences. If you have not talked to a group before, check with someone who has. A friend or colleague who has already lectured to the same group can help you know what to expect.

Important questions to ask yourself: **"What do students already know about my topic?"** and **"What do they need to know?"** If many students know the lecture subject, you will want to reveal your credentials. Conversely, if they know much less about the topic than you do, your challenge changes—you'll want to avoid talking down to them. By carefully analyzing the needs and characteristics of students, you can assure your comments arrive at the appropriate level.

After you assess the students and you write appropriate student-centered learning objectives, it's time to collect and arrange your information. What you already know and what you learn from others or from books will probably yield more information than you have time to present. Additional information is especially important in the informal lecture, when students ask questions, but don't overlook its value in the formal lecture. Students will expect the instructor to know more about the topic than he or she can present in one lecture.

In preparing the lecture, follow a lesson-planning process. Choose an appropriate organizational pattern. Effectively use support material. Have a clear introduction and a complete conclusion. These basic building blocks will facilitate student understanding and retention. The major concerns of lesson planning are more or less common with all methods, but some are of special importance to the lecture.

Developing the Lecture

A well-organized lecture contributes to learning by appealing to students, giving them a reason to listen, and providing a forecast of what will be taught. Strong organization and clear verbal and visual support in the body of the lesson help students understand and retain material. A complete conclusion to the lesson will help you teach, challenge, reinforce, and leave the students with a satisfying sense of completeness.

Each of these concerns becomes especially critical since the burden for presenting the lecture falls squarely on the instructor. In fact, every part of the lecture must be designed to capture attention and challenge students to listen. Anything less will cost you the engagement of your audience.

Selecting Audiovisual Resources and Tools

Careful planning can help you choose appropriate and timely audiovisual tools and resources. The following guidelines should help:

- **Use only relevant materials**. Avoid using materials solely for aesthetic or entertainment value. Visual materials should certainly be interesting, but remember the primary purpose of any visual aid: to portray or support an idea graphically. Irrelevant materials distract from the ideas you present.

- **Use visual materials large enough to be seen by all the students.** Have you ever been annoyed by being seated in the back of the room where you couldn't see the visuals? As you prepare for your presentation, display the visuals you want to use, and then stand where your most distant student will be. If you can't easily read the material, replace it with something more appropriate.

- **Use visual materials only at the proper time**. Materials made visible too soon or that remain in view long after the point has been made distract from the lecture. Also, don't show a full list of 10 main points for the students and then discuss each one. Instead, uncover the points one at a time. This holds students' attention.

- **Keep visual materials as simple and clear as possible**. Emphasize only the most important information. Omit unnecessary details. Your audience prefers a series of simple charts to a single, complicated one.

- **Talk to the students, not to the visual aid.** As you explain a chart, look at your students as often as possible. At the time you make your presentation, you should be so familiar with your visual aids that you won't need to constantly look at them. When possible, paraphrase the visual and explain its relevance instead of simply reading it.

- **Place visuals away from obstructions.** Make sure objects or persons don't obstruct the view of your students.

Selecting a Method of Presentation

When presenting a lecture, instructors have four basic options: (1) speaking from memory; (2) reading from a manuscript; (3) speaking impromptu, without specific preparation; and (4) speaking extemporaneously with a great deal of preparation and limited notes. The fourth method, which allows instructors the most freedom in adjusting to students' reaction, is probably best suited for teaching at the college or university level.

Memorizing—Want to put an audience to sleep? Memorize a speech and deliver it. This is the poorest method of delivering lectures, so use it sparingly. The memorized lecture is a straitjacket. It cannot be adapted to fit student reactions, and it's almost sure to destroy spontaneity and a sense of communication. Memorization also requires a lot of preparation . . . and the danger of forgetting is ever-present.

Reading—Reading a lecture from a manuscript allows a speaker to plan the exact words and phrases to use, but its disadvantages may outweigh the advantages. Many new college instructors use the manuscript as a crutch instead of fully thinking through the ideas and the ways they can be effectively communicated in a lecture. All too often, the written lecture is regarded simply as an essay to be read aloud. It can quickly become too broad, or be filled with language too abstract to be understood. And there's this—very few people can read from a manuscript with the same emphasis and spontaneity used with extemporaneous delivery. Reading can result in a flat, dry, staged performance.

Impromptu Speaking—Impromptu speaking requires a tremendous amount of skill and deep knowledge. It may be necessary at times to lecture on the spur of the moment without preparation, but only the most seasoned and experienced instructors who are masters of their subjects should rely on this method. When you use impromptu speaking, remember to:

- Keep spoken words simple, clear, and vivid.

- Make sentences short and ideas descriptive.

- Transition between thoughts and ideas.

- Provide punctuation using your vocal inflection, variety, and pauses.

- Use repetition to emphasize main ideas and key points.

- Use direct address when speaking about people. Personal pronouns such as *I, we, our, us,* and *you* are better than *they, people, a person, the reader,* or *the listener.*

- Use concrete language where possible. Follow abstract or complicated reasoning with specific examples, comparisons, and definitions.

- If you have notes, prepare them to facilitate reading. It may help to double—or triple-space your notes, mark the manuscript, use only one side of the paper, increase the font size of the print, and use short paragraphs.

- Rehearse your thoughts aloud several times to hear how they sound. Record them, if you like. You'll discover places where you might communicate more effectively.

- Try to make your lecture sound conversational.

- Practice looking at your audience most of the time. And trust yourself. Even the most seasoned and experienced instructors fall back on thoughts and phrases they have used before. They have spent years, so to speak, preparing to give an unprepared lesson.

Extemporaneous Speaking—This technique is used most widely by successful and effective college instructors. It produces the best results when it is preceded by full preparation and adequate practice. (Mark Twain once said, "The best extemporaneous speech I ever gave took me two weeks to prepare.") The lesson is carefully planned and outlined in detail, but the instructor's only guide is a well-constructed outline. Think of it as a lesson planned idea by idea, rather than word by word.

A well-planned outline brings an instructor many advantages. The outline compels instructors to organize ideas. It drives the speaker to weigh materials in advance. It frees the speaker to adapt a lesson to the occasion and to adjust to student reactions. It enables instructors to change what they plan to say right up to the last moment. In short, it permits the instructor to adhere to the two vital needs of effective teaching: preparation and practice.

<u>Presenting the Lecture</u>

Preparing a lecture can be laborious. But for many instructors, the hardest part is still to come—actually presenting it. Questions instructors most often ask? *How many notes should I use? How can I overcome nervousness? What kind of physical behavior is appropriate when I speak? What if my voice isn't suited to speaking before a group? How can I project sincerity and enthusiasm? What can I do to encourage student interaction?*

Dealing With Your Nervousness—If you suffer from stage fright, nervousness, or fear of speaking, you're like most of us. Public speaking may be the most common phobia in our culture. It probably doesn't help to know that your own anxiety may cause your students to become uneasy or edgy. Rest assured that some nervousness is both natural and desirable. Even skilled instructors often feel butterflies when they step to the lectern. As a person new to teaching, you may find that practicing a lecture several times, preferably in the room where the lecture will be given, is helpful. Rehearsal reminds us to concentrate on the pronunciation of a new word or to check an additional piece of information on an important point. Consider other suggestions for overcoming nervousness:

- **Be enthusiastic**. At times we may lecture on subjects we initially find dull, but as we get more involved, the subject grows more interesting. The more enthusiasm you show for the subject, the more the students will engage with you and what you are saying. Remember, there is no such thing as a dull subject—only dull college instructors.

- **Hold good thoughts toward your students.** Those students in the audience? They're the same ones you enjoy speaking with in a less structured environment. Most classes are made up of adult learners who have an interest in your subject. Students do not come to class to boo the instructor or throw vegetables. Most have great respect for their instructors. They want you to do a good job.

- **Don't rush.** Sometimes new college instructors are so anxious to get started they begin before they are ready. Take a little extra time to arrange your notes. It will pay big dividends. When you are ready to start, look at the various parts of the class, take a deep breath, and begin to speak.

- **Be funny.** Humor relaxes the instructor and students, especially at the beginning of a lecture, and it places the instructor directly in communication with the students. Humor reclaims students' attention, and it emphasizes important points. A humorous story or anecdote may be the most powerful memory or clarification device a speaker can use. But humor must be used properly to be effective.

Here are five good tips for using humor:

- **Know the item thoroughly**—If you know the story and have told it before, you will be able to tell it again and know the response to expect. A good rule to follow? Don't use a story or humorous item unless you have repeated it several times in informal situations. This lets you practice and also gauge the reactions of others.

- **Don't use off-color stories to get a cheap laugh**—Even people who laugh at such stories in private often lose respect for the instructor who uses them in public.

- **Vitalize humor**—Stories should be personalized so they are believable—so they sound as if they really happened. Rather than talk about "this guy I heard about" or "this truck driver," give names to characters in your stories. Successful comedians and speakers always vitalize their humor.

- **Don't laugh before the audience laughs**—If you fail to get the story across, laughing alone on a platform is disastrous. If the joke fails, leave it and go on.

- **Capitalize on the unexpected**—A primary element of humor? People laugh when they are surprised. Quips, puns, exaggeration, and understatement all can help you.

Pacing the Lecture—Transitions signal to students that the lecture is progressing to a new point. Transitions are also important in maintaining the continuity of the information. Consider this sample transition: **"We have discussed the reasons for standardized tests for entry into the MBA program. Next we will consider the benefits of such a program."** Notice how this transition indicates a change in direction, but does not indicate the reason for the change, or its importance.

For transitions to be effective, they should (1) mention the point previously discussed; (2) relate that point to the learning objective; and (3) introduce the next point. Suppose the objective is for students to know why standardized tests qualify them for entry into a school's MBA program. Notice how the following transition incorporates all three transition steps: **"(1) We have discussed the reasons why standardized tests are used as criteria for entry into the school's MBA program, (2) but these reasons alone will not prove a need for such a program. To understand that need more fully, (3) we must next examine, in several practical situations, the benefits of standardized tests as they pertain to the school's MBA program."** When planned and used correctly, transitions contribute substantially to the continuity of the total lecture. Without them, a lecture sounds choppy and fragmented. Put transitions into your lesson plan for a lecture.

Interim summaries are useful tools for maintaining continuity in a lecture and also for highlighting areas of particular importance. You don't always need summaries between main points—if the point is very clear, a summary may be redundant and boring. Use summaries when main points are unusually long or contain complex, unfamiliar information. Repeat the information concisely to reinforce understanding before you present fresh information. Summaries provide a means to progress logically from one main point through a transition and into the next point.

The summary given in the lecture's conclusion should be designed so that it reviews the aspects of a concept or principle you consider particularly important. Think of your summary as the headlines from

41

the lecture. Relate key ideas to each other and to the lesson objective. It's your bottom-line opportunity to reinforce critical aspects of the lesson.

Did you know that questions add continuity to the lesson? Plan some rhetorical questions to set off a main point or at the conclusion of the lecture. Questions encourage students to review the information they've heard in their own minds. Questions also indicate areas of special importance; phrase questions to allow students to see the relationship of key areas to the lesson objective.

<u>Managing Your Physical Behavior</u>

Communication experts tell us that more than half of our meanings may be communicated nonverbally. As illustrated in Figure 2, some nonverbal meaning is communicated through vocal cues; a great deal of meaning is conveyed through eye contact, body movement, and gestures. You will benefit greatly from knowing how physical behavior can improve your lecturing skill.

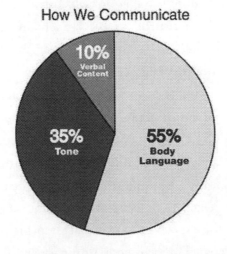

Model of How We Communicate

Eye Contact—Nothing will enhance your delivery more than effective eye contact with your students. First, it lets the students know you are interested in them; most people like others to look at them when talking. Second, effective eye contact allows you to receive nonverbal feedback from your students. With good eye contact, you can gauge the effect of your remarks and determine if you are being understood. You can detect which points make an impact and which do not. Eye contact cues you to adjust your rate of delivery or to emphasize, rephrase, or summarize certain points . . . or even to add more supporting data. Third, effective eye contact enhances your credibility; students judge instructors with greater eye contact as being more competent.

To achieve genuine eye contact, you must do more than merely look in the direction of your students. You must have an earnest desire to communicate with them. The old advice of looking over the tops of your students' heads or attempting to look at all parts of the class systematically simply doesn't cut it. Similarly, looking at only one part of the audience or directing attention only to those students who provide positive feedback may cause you to ignore larger parts of the audience. Make it evident to each person in a small class, and each part of the audience in larger auditoriums, that you are interested in them as individuals and are eager to have them understand the ideas you present.

What is effective eye contact? It's direct and impartial. Look directly into the eyes of your students and look impartially at all parts of the audience, not just at a chosen few.

Body Movement—Body movement is one of the most important factors of dynamic and meaningful physical behavior. Purposeful body movement helps hold the attention needed for learning to occur. Movement also represents a marked departure or change in your delivery pattern; it is a convenient way of punctuating your message. Students can see you are done with one idea or line of thought and ready to transition to the next. And body movement helps you as the instructor by working off nervous energy that might find an outlet in nervous tics or other distracting behaviors.

How much movement is desirable? Unless the formality of the situation or the need to use a fixed microphone keeps you in one position, you should feel free to move frequently when presenting a lecture. Movement from behind the lectern can reduce the psychological distance between you and your students, putting them more at ease. Some instructors feel they need the lectern to hold their notes. Instruction is actually more effective if you carry your notes with you instead of looking down at the lectern to see them.

When you look at your notes, remember to *direct your eyes (not your head) to the paper.*

Some instructors do move too much, pacing restlessly in front of the class. Still others have awkward movements that do not help communication. Some leave their notes on the lectern, and then move in and out from behind it, which is distracting. Other instructors plant their feet firmly in one place, then rock side to side in regular cadence.

Feel free to move around the class and don't be constrained by the lectern. Move with reason and purpose, punctuating points, directing attention, and facilitating learning.

Gestures—Gestures are most effective when purposeful and used to help clarify or emphasize ideas in the lecture. Fidgeting with a paper clip, shuffling papers, and scratching your ear are not gestures—they distract from the verbal message. Placing both hands in your pockets, behind your back, or in front of you in the fig-leaf position severely limits the way you can use them for gesturing. Holding your shoulders and head in one position during the entire lecture also robs you of an effective means of strengthening your communication.

Act naturally. Gestures will be most effective if you make a conscious effort to relax your muscles before you speak. Take a few short steps or unobtrusively arrange your notes. Many speakers begin to gesture, but perhaps out of fear, they stop. Fear doesn't help you sell your ideas.

As with all aspects of communication, gestures must fit the situation. A standard gesture does not fit all subjects and situations. The larger the audience, the more pronounced the gestures will need to be. Be natural—don't try to adopt a dynamic mode of delivery if by nature you are quiet and reserved. Your movement should feel purposeful, but spontaneous. A good practice is to watch people talking with each other in a small group; try to bring the same naturalness and spontaneity of gesture to your lecture.

Use of Voice—Your lecturing voice should be pleasant, easily understood, and should express differences in meaning. Think of these properties as quality, intelligibility, and variety.

- **Quality**—A pleasing quality or tone is a basic component of a good speaking voice. While basic aspects of your voice are difficult to change, your voice may become weaker when you are excited, tense when you feel suspense, or resonant as you read solemn language. Vocal quality can convey sincerity and enthusiasm. Students can often tell from the voice if the instructor feels happy, angry, sad, fearful, or confident. Be aware of the effect your attitude and emotion have on your lecture.

- **Intelligibility**—Attention to articulation, pronunciation, and volume will help make your voice more intelligible. Avoid vocalized pauses, stock expressions, and substandard grammar, which all detract from your voice being intelligible.

  o **Articulation or Enunciation**—Good articulation comes from the jaw, tongue, and lips. Most articulation

45

problems result from laziness of the tongue and lips or failure to open the mouth wide enough. You should over-articulate rather than under-articulate speech sounds. What sounds like over-articulation to you will come out as crisp, understandable words and phrases to your students.

o **Pronunciation**—Educated people in your community, as well as national radio and television announcers, provide a good standard for pronunciation. Remember that pronunciation acceptable in informal conversation may be substandard in a lecture . . . but don't overcompensate with unnaturally formal diction.

o **Filler Phrases**—This refers to vocalized pauses such as "a," "uh," "um," and "ah," often used at the beginning of a sentence. While a few vocalized pauses are natural and acceptable, too many filler phrases can distract. Avoid overused expressions, such as "OK," "like," and "you know." These serve little positive purpose and may convey a lack of knowledge, preparation, and confidence.

o **Grammar**—Substandard grammar has no place in teaching at the college or university level. It reduces instructor credibility with students. Research shows that even students who have been using substandard grammar all of their lives can, with diligent practice, make significant gains in this area in a relatively short time.

○ **Variety**—Students get bored listening to an instructor with a monotonous delivery style. Having an intelligible voice isn't enough; you need to vary your vocal tone and focus on the fundamentals such as rate, volume, force, pitch, and emphasis. Most instructors speak at a rate of 120 to 180 words a minute during a lecture. In normal speech, we vary the rate—it changes a great deal even within the 120—to 180-word-per-minute range. Here's an example—a new college instructor teaching a class for the first time may speak at a rapid rate all the time. A seasoned instructor who has taught a course several times generally speaks at a slower rate. Varying the rate of delivery not only conveys ideas, it also emphasizes feelings. A slower rate may be appropriate for presenting main points, while a more rapid rate may lend itself to support material. An occasional well-timed pause punctuates thought and emphasizes ideas; a dramatic pause at the proper time may also express feelings and ideas as effectively as words.

○ **Volume**—Make sure everyone can hear you, but don't be too bombastic if you're in a small room. You need force or vocal energy at times to emphasize and dramatize ideas; a drowsy audience will quickly come to attention if the instructor uses the voice forcefully.

○ **Pitch**—A higher-pitched voice carries better than a lower-pitched one. On the other hand, students tire faster listening to a higher-pitched voice. If your voice falls within normal limits, neither too high nor too low, work for variety when you speak. Try not to become too firmly entrenched in your habitual pitch level.

○ **Emphasis**—Use emphasis wisely. Avoid overemphasis or continual emphasis, as emphasizing a point beyond its real value may cause you to appear insincere.

Projecting Sincerity

You need to prepare well and possess strong delivery skills to do an effective job in the classroom, but you also need something more.

You must be sincere.

Students can be amazingly tolerant of weakness in both preparation and delivery, but if they doubt your sincerity, the game is over. You lose credibility. And once you have lost credibility, you're no longer an effective instructor.

Sincerity is reflected in your eye contact, enthusiasm, and concern for your students. It's crucial to seem involved and interested in the subject or topic of the lecture and to clearly demonstrate confidence that you are doing the best job possible in the classroom.

Encouraging Student Interaction

When presenting a lecture, student interaction can best be encouraged in two ways. First, students ask questions to clarify confusing points or to ensure their understanding of the information. Second, the instructor asks the students questions to stimulate thinking. By asking both planned and spontaneous questions, the instructor can stimulate participation, emphasize important points, and, most importantly, judge whether students understand the material.

To be most effective, student interaction should occur consistently throughout a lecture. Allow ample time for questions and answers when planning and practicing the lesson. At the beginning of your lecture, encourage students to ask questions. Students will be more likely to participate if the instructor indicates through direct eye contact, frequent pauses, and a relaxed delivery that he or she is sincerely interested in student participation. Instructor questions are especially effective when they require students to summarize important information or to provide additional support in the form of personal examples.

Although robust student interaction contributes to learning, it should not take priority over achieving the lesson objectives. If a portion of the material is complex, unfamiliar to the students, or follows a necessary sequence, questions may be distracting or cause confusion. In this case, you should ask students to hold their comments until the difficult material has been presented. This may also be necessary in the event of time constraints near the end of a lecture. Plan carefully to ensure a comfortable balance between course material and questions.

<u>Summary</u>

The lecture is one of the most popular teaching methods in colleges and universities. Advantages of the lecture method are: (1) it allows for the presentation of many ideas in a short time; (2) it is suitable for introducing a subject; (3) it is convenient for teaching large groups; (4) it is valuable for supplementing material from other sources; and (5) it allows for a large number of students to hear an expert.

Disadvantages of the lecture method are: (1) it is not appropriate for certain types of learning; (2) it requires a lot of instructor preparation; (3) it depends greatly on the instructor's communication skill; (4) it limits ways for the instructor to estimate student progress; and (5) it limits active participation by students.

To prepare for a lecture, analyze your student audience, carefully plan the beginning and ending of the lecture, and choose audiovisual support materials to help students listen and understand. You should consider using humor when appropriate, and plan transitions and summaries as needed.

When presenting your lecture, master your nervousness; pay attention to eye contact, body movement, and gestures; and strive for a pleasant, communicative, and expressive voice. Most importantly, show sincerity toward your students, your subject, and yourself at all times.

Chapter 4

Case Study Method

I'm a true believer in case studies. You may be too, if you've ever been part of a really well prepared, relevant case study experience.

A few years ago, I worked for months to develop a case study for a Public Human Resources Management course that I teach at Troy University. That case study, <u>A Day in the Life of a City Manager</u>, required exhaustive research. I conducted interviews, delved into an actual strategic plan for a mid-sized city, and made a close reading of a great deal of existing material on the subject. I was very proud of the final product.

One of my graduate students worked at the time as an assistant city manager for a small city in central Georgia. He had what I call a <u>shining</u>—he was ambitious and bright, with his eyes on self-betterment and bigger goals. The case study mirrored very closely the reality of his day-to-day challenges on the job.

"The course reminded me at every stage of the situations I faced virtually any day of the week in the real world back in my town," he said. "The

exercises really honed my decision-making skills and solidly equipped me to deal with tough issues confronting most every city manager."

My student took the training seriously, absorbed its lessons fully. Then came a payoff.

"I give the case study a large measure of credit for the job offer I received in less than a year to be city manager in a municipality a state away," he said. "Going through that case study powerfully boosted my confidence on the job as well as my actual performance. Also, it obviously boosted my marketability."

A well-done case study reminds one of the old adage: <u>One picture is worth a thousand words.</u>

Sometimes one hands-on experience with the elements of a real-world situation teaches a lesson more effectively than all the text in a semester of lectures.

<u>Introduction</u>

The case study method confronts students with real-life challenges. Bridging the gap in the classroom between theory and practice, it presents a real-world situation that requires analysis and problem-solving drawing on previously learned concepts and principles. The case study also serves as a basis for class discussion. Because a case describes a problem already faced by others in a given field, it challenges students to apply what they know and comprehend to a situation they may likely face in the world beyond the classroom.

The case study method takes students out of the passive role and makes them partners with the instructor in applying the concepts and principles they study. The method allows students to think, reason, and use data in a logical fashion, just as they would in an actual work environment. Variations of the case study method first appeared in the teaching of medicine and law, but over the years case studies have been widely used in the study of business, management, and education—almost any area rich with cases from real situations.

Types of Cases

We find four main types of cases: conflict management, problem-solving, decision-making, and crisis intervention.

Conflict Management—A conflict management case contains all the information the student will need to deal with a situation, and it requires access to no other sources. Business school cases, for instance, often illustrate a real situation faced by managers in the past. Conflict management cases describe the problem to be addressed, how the problem arose, the organization's structure, the people involved in the situation, and their perceptions at the time of the incident.

Conflict management cases may extend to great length and take considerable time to analyze. Some programs make the case study the basis of an entire course. Students read the case, perform an analysis, make a decision, and support that decision before their peers. The instructor evaluates the students' ability to analyze, develop insight, and make a decision.

In some instances, the conflict management case may be abbreviated. Since it is shorter, the focus tightens and the solution or solutions may be more limited. The abbreviated case may deal with one problem, or it may outline a scenario with a series of limited choices.

Problem-Solving Case—In this type of case study, students receive limited information about a situation, and their work includes finding the additional information they need. The instructor presents a brief

53

scenario and charges students to take some action, make a decision, or suggest recommendations. The instructor usually provides additional information *only* as students request it. Providing students a partial text of the case helps them develop analytical and problem-solving skills. It also helps them learn how to ask the right kinds of questions. The incident they study, along with the processing of the case, prepares students for the contingencies they may face in an actual work environment, where decisions based on partial information are often the norm.

Decision-Making Case—In the decision-making case, students again receive limited information. They must obtain additional data from outside the classroom, return to class and ask for new information, or receive another segment of the case from the instructor, then return to interaction, and so on. Additional readings, interviews, and library and/or Internet research provide facts and context. Think of the process as similar to conducting a research project—an artful blend of dealing with reality while acquiring additional knowledge and skills. One exciting and effective approach I've seen involves presenting all the data required by students at one time but in an unorganized form (simulating an e-mail in-box exercise). Extraneous information may be included, training students to select and arrange information into some meaningful pattern for action.

Crisis Intervention Case—The crisis intervention case resembles the problem-solving and decision-making cases. Students receive limited information. The situation unfolds in installments. At the end of each, students decide whether intervention is called for at that point. Some incidents resolve themselves, and intervention will only aggravate the situation. Other incidents continue to deteriorate and might even become irresolvable if students don't intervene at the right time. The sequential case lends itself particularly well to MBA or law school students.

Benefits of the Case Study Method

The case study method provides students with experience and skills in solving actual problems. Many students can repeat isolated facts or principles, but have difficulty relating these facts and principles to new situations. As they learn problem-solving techniques through case studies, students make their mistakes in the classroom . . . not on the job, where errors prove more costly.

Students also gain experience making decisions and working with colleagues. By interacting with fellow students, they learn to respect the opinions and judgments of others.

Importantly, case studies teach something else. *There isn't always one right answer.* Since the case may not list all pertinent facts, students learn to cope with ambiguity and uncertainty.

Various Ways to Use the Case Study

With its versatility, the case study method lends itself to a wide variety of teaching conditions. It can be the basis of an entire curriculum, a full course, or a single lesson. Still, it may not be suitable in every situation, especially with new undergraduate students or with large classes. It is not applicable where students need to learn a procedure or a single solution that has been accepted as correct. Moreover, case studies do not lend themselves to developing objectives at the knowledge level of learning. (The lecture method and reading usually prove more efficient.) But once the knowledge level has been achieved, the case study offers an excellent way for students to progress to the higher levels of learning—application, synthesis, or evaluation.

There are three basic ways to use a case study: complete course method, capstone method, and problem-solving method.

Complete Course Method—Some colleges and universities use the case study method exclusively, especially in their graduate business programs. Instructors assume that the best way to prepare for a business career is to have experience in analyzing data and making decisions. Students in these courses receive complex cases to analyze and solve. The quality of the analysis and the reasoning behind decisions often matter more than arriving at a single solution. In the classroom, students participate in collective analysis and decision-making. With more and more experience analyzing cases, students begin to form generalizations they can apply to all new situations. Case studies in this way substitute for on-the-job training.

Normally in the case study course, concepts and principles are not taught directly.

Instead, they emerge gradually as students formulate theories to support decisions. Because they learn theories from practical work with problems, students remember them better and recall them more fully in real-world situations.

The case study course is usually conducted using group problem-solving techniques in open-class sessions. But the case may also be an out-of-class written assignment, with students bringing solutions to class along with rationale for their decisions. Solutions may form the basis for class discussion or be turned in for the instructor to grade. Such variations may overcome the need for relatively small classes.

Capstone Method—Some schools use a case or a series of cases at the end of a particular program—a capstone—to see how well students apply course content. Often, a case will be preceded by lectures, discussions, and other types of instruction. Students will then be required to apply what they have learned to a series of cases specifically designed to support course objectives. This capstone method is particularly appropriate when students start at the knowledge or comprehension level of learning and are brought gradually to the application level.

In some graduate school programs, where previous courses, lessons, readings, and lectures have supplied basic material, case studies can be used to give students an opportunity to apply course theory.

The Problem-Solving Method—Some college instructors use case studies to help their students develop problem-solving skills. Employing a very focused but realistic problem situation as a vehicle, an instructor plans the lesson much like a guided discussion. An example? Let's say the objective of the lesson is to have students comprehend a principle of management called "division of work." The instructor might introduce a case-study situation in which a supervisor failed to take this principle into account, lowering morale and raising absence and turnover.

The case study, used as a problem-solving or skill-building exercise, isn't always after a "correct" solution to the problem posed. It's more important that students understand the assessment and decision-making principles involved. The problem should be sufficiently interesting and difficult to involve all students. Because the written problem provides a discussion vehicle, the class can also be broken up into smaller discussion groups.

A variation of the short case can also be used in group dynamics exercises where the emphasis is on team-building. Similarly, the short case can be used to demonstrate a decision-making process where understanding the process matters more than identifying a solution.

Planning to Teach the Case

Proper use of the case study method requires a good deal of preparation, presentation, and follow-up. Consider several best practices:

Identify the specific learning objective for the class and evaluate the relationship between the lesson and the rest of the curriculum. For example, if you have taught the principles of management to students during a two-week period and now you want to see if the students can apply these principles to a given situation, using the case as a "capstone method" will help reinforce and extend previous lectures. Many top graduate business schools use this approach.

Before the actual lesson planning begins, the instructor must select some logical sequence for analyzing the case. An analytic format will often be inherent in the case's concept, principle, or objective. If so, these main points become the procedures the students will use to develop the lesson, and they also might be used as broad categories in class discussions.

As you introduce the case study lesson plan, include an overview explaining the course learning objectives and their relationship to the case. The students should have an opportunity to read the case before coming to class, and they should be told how the lesson will proceed and the point of view they should adopt. Lastly, students should be informed in advance if the case will involve any role-play.

The body of the case study lesson plan should elaborate on each main point in the lesson and include well-formed, preplanned questions. Examples of effective questions that should be built into the lesson plan:

- **"What are the facts in this case?"**

- **"Who is causing the biggest problem?"**

- **"Which of these violations has the most serious consequences?"**

If you prepare thoroughly, you will be able to transition from one main point to another and from issue to issue within main points. You can guide the class into critical areas for discussion, and ultimately lead them to the overall lesson objective.

A conclusion section of the lesson plan summarizes the case, adds additional information, and relates it to the concept or principle you wish to illustrate. The conclusion also shows how this same concept or principle can be useful in dealing with similar situations.

Selecting a Case to Teach

You may not be able find the exact kind of case to achieve a specific objective. But there's a solution—write your own case to fit the specific need. The idea for a case may come from a current event, an article, or from your personal experience.

You will find abundant case studies in a number of great sources. The Harvard Business School, through the Intercollegiate Case Clearing House, offers a centralized source of prepared cases. You may order cases from the published catalog, for a nominal fee. The library at your college or university may also have an extensive collection of cases used by other instructors. Local community libraries and the Internet are great sources.

In evaluating a case for use, ask yourself five important questions:

1. **Is the case realistic?** Fabricated cases may lack credibility. If the case is not realistic, will students take it seriously? Will their solutions, decisions, or actions seem real? While it's possible to invent a case or use a composite of several situations, such an approach is rarely as successful as dealing with a real-life case.

2. **Is the case meaningful?** The case should be meaningful to students. They should identify with it in some way. They must be generally familiar with the problem either through past experience or in the experiences they expect to face in the

future. A case about a space shuttle accident, for instance, may not work for students who are not involved with space travel or who do not have the necessary technical background.

3. **Is the case challenging?** The case should contain an actual conflict or potential controversy. Don't choose a case with an obvious solution.

4. **Is the case complete?** The case should present enough information to let students deal with its problems without referring to outside sources.

5. **Does the case provide for a logical difference of opinion?** A case study that prompts a single line of analysis may not result in productive educational discussion. The most effective cases provide an opportunity for reasonable people to differ.

Developing a Case Study Teaching Strategy

A good case allows both the instructor and student to achieve educational objectives. It should enable the instructor to reinforce general principles with specific examples, and it should help students learn from the past by analyzing a close-to-real-life situation. You can increase your odds of successfully teaching a case if you develop a case facilitation strategy beforehand.

What's in a case study teaching strategy? It includes essential details about the case such as major issues, case characters, character personalities, relationships, goals and values, case prerequisites, and key questions to guide discussion. (Note that the teaching strategy is <u>not</u> the solution to the case. It's the instructor's notes that detail typical student activities the case will stimulate, and that define the specific student outcomes you expect.) The teaching strategy should also define the student level for which the case is written and how to relate the case to readings and to preceding or subsequent classes. The notes should include at least an outline of the instructor's personal analysis of the case, to show where it might differ from student analysis.

After writing the teaching strategy, you may find that the case contains insufficient or misleading information. If so, revise or amend it before giving the case to students. For certain groups, the case may assume knowledge of a process or background material you'll need to summarize in an attachment. A case on racial discrimination in promotion, for instance, may depend on a detailed knowledge of Title VII of the Civil Rights Act of 1964 and subsequent cases and laws. The average student may not have this knowledge.

Finally, the case study teaching strategy should extend beyond the limits of the case. You should be prepared to include legal, political, economic, or social information, and also know policies and procedures in effect at the time of the case. You may need to explain concepts and principles alluded to but not defined in the case. The more knowledge and expertise you have, the greater the chance of teaching the case effectively.

Facilitating the Case

Although there is no set procedure for facilitating case studies, the following practices will contribute to the method's effectiveness and help students achieve the learning objectives:

- **Refrain from lecturing**—The case method is inherently a student-centered approach. Keep your comments to a minimum. Let the students do the talking.

- **Guide the discussion**—Some instructors begin with the question, **"What is the issue here?"** then go on to **"What are the pertinent facts?"** Others begin with the more general question, **"What action should be taken?"** Your approach depends on your students and the subject matter.

- **Manage participation**—The case discussion is controlled much like the guided discussion, except here you have more freedom to enter the discussion. Keep track of the discussion and provide a visual record that helps the class see where the discussion has been and where it is going. Also use questions to stimulate thinking. The questioning techniques used in the case method are the same as for a guided discussion.

- **Direct traffic, but don't be a driver**—Remember, there is no single right answer in a case study. It is more profitable and effective to lead students toward sound application of principles than to persist in an endless search for a perfect solution. In the body of the lesson, facilitate the discussion. Do not impose your views, pass judgment on contributions, or argue with students who differ with your point of view. Remember your role—to encourage independent thinking and achieve the overall lesson objective.

Diversifying Mode of Presentation

To this point, we have assumed that all cases are written. While the majority of cases do appear in written format, other modes of presentation can add variety, drama, and realism to the class. Movies, videos, and vignettes can powerfully convey the dramatic emotions inherent in a case. Typically, a video will unfold the situation to a decision point; then the students take over. After the students have made a decision, the video case study can be continued by presenting more information, or by using the outcome as a basis for further discussion. Another variation? Have a live presentation in which the participants recreate the case experiences for the class, then respond to questions. As an alternative, the students can meet with the case participant, perhaps in the actual case environment. This increases the realism immensely; how the original participants saw the case is often more critical than the interpretations of these perceptions by a case writer.

Monitoring the Rules of Engagement

Both the instructor and students have defined roles in making the case study a profitable and successful lesson. Your role? Again, don't dominate, control, structure the discussion, or provide your own solution. Simply guide and involve students in the discussion and solution of the case. You also serve as the recorder, questioner, and occasionally as a clarifier.

Instructor's Role—Provide direction and organization to the discussion of a case by writing ideas on a board as students submit them. Also record problem areas and items for further analysis and solutions by the discussion group. To avoid confusion or distraction, you might list the major elements of the selected decision or analysis process on the board. Under each category, you might list specific student contributions. This requires disciplined listening and undivided attention to every statement made during discussion.

During the discussion:

- Ask good questions. Questions are the primary technique for clarifying contributions to the discussion and for relating ideas.

- Encourage students to apply past experiences to the new situation presented in the case.

- Record student assertions and stimulate more disciplined problem analysis.

- Assure that the discussion is meaningful and that every student has an opportunity to participate.

- Establish good rapport and maintain student interest in the case.

What you do after the class session is often as important as what you did beforehand. If student participation is part of the course grade, tell your students the criteria for grading and take notes while the impressions are still fresh in your mind. For future use of the case, review the lesson plan and note needed corrections, possible changes in questions, and new lines of thought or different methods of analysis brought out by the students. This keeps the case fresh and makes it a more refined tool for subsequent classes.

Students' Role—The case method of instruction usually requires more student preparation than any other teaching method. If students do not prepare for class participation, they do themselves an injustice and deprive other students of possible learning experiences. As minimum preparation, students must read and study the case thoroughly. If there is time, they might also refer to as many related references as possible.

During class discussion of the case, students should think reflectively and strive for cooperation rather than competition. They should each contribute briefly and directly to the discussion and should assist in developing group concepts. Self-motivation is a significant element of the case study method.

Summary

The case study method, properly used, initiates students into the ways of independent thinking and responsible judgment. It makes students tackle work-related situations and places them in an active role, open to constructive criticism from all sides. The case study method also puts the burden of understanding and judgment on students and gives them the opportunity to make contributions to learning.

In the problem-solving environment of the classroom, students develop communication skills, contributing to ideas offered by other members of the group or even taking exception to peers' ideas. Both actions require effective communication techniques and involve interaction that leads to consensus and understanding. The case study method increases students' ability to appreciate other points of view, to explore and discuss differences of opinion, and to reach an agreement. It forces students to think analytically, constructively, and creatively, and gives them the satisfaction of participating in a disciplined problem-solving activity with fellow students.

Chapter 5

Teaching Interview Method

Instructors can find many opportunities to talk about the things they know. Personally, I have always enjoyed the teaching interview as a means of teaching a subject. Here's why.

When I prepare a traditional lecture, I assemble my information in perfect ranks and order. I'm as efficient as an Air Force general, and when I step in front of the classroom, the facts fly.

Still sometimes, despite my very best efforts and energy, I wonder if I'm on automatic pilot just a bit. The facts I'm teaching haven't changed. History hasn't changed. Maybe I haven't changed either. Does that sense of stasis give students the slightest subconscious hint that the subject matter isn't really to be taken seriously?

The teaching interview offers a fresher approach to passing along valuable information. It's a bit tricky, at times—Murphy's Law can run wild in the unscripted interview. But so can spontaneous stories, personal anecdotes and surprising information that teach in unrehearsed, eye-opening ways.

When I am interviewed as an instructor, or when I instruct a class through the teaching interview, I sense an energy that brings students out of the occasional humdrum of scholastics and into the learning moment.

The teaching interview engages. Engagement means listening. Listening, of course, leads to learning.

Introduction

A teaching interview is a special type of controlled conversation aimed at achieving specific learning objectives. Think of it as a dialogue in an educational setting. The interview pairs the primary instructor with a recognized subject matter expert, and students learn by observing and asking questions.

Benefits of the Teaching Interview Method

Creativity—The teaching interview is a creative way to facilitate adult learning. This method can prove particularly effective when used to supplement the instructor's knowledge of a specific subject area or to cover a particularly broad subject. For example, students in a business course would greatly benefit from the interview of an expert with experience in acquisitions and mergers. Attorneys who have been involved in major cases contribute significantly to an understanding of the judicial process. So professors teaching in graduate schools and professional education programs like law school and medical school frequently bring experts to the classroom and interview them for their courses. The teaching interview provides a welcome change of pace, adding variety to the curriculum.

Credibility—The teaching interview effectively increases the instructor's credibility and enhances the course, program, and school's brand. By bringing an expert into the classroom, the instructor acknowledges he or she is not the expert or authority in a certain area. The instructor's job instead becomes questioning the expert in a way that allows the students to learn. In using an expert, the instructor shows students that achievement of the lesson objectives ranks higher than the instructor's ego.

Flexibility—The teaching interview is one of the most flexible teaching methods and can be used in a variety of ways. It breaks the monotony of the course, keeping students engaged. It effectively introduces or presents a case study. It can be used as a problem-solving activity, in which the instructor presents a problem for the expert to discuss.

Planning for the Teaching Interview

First, as always, examine the lesson closely to determine if the teaching interview is your most appropriate method to help students achieve the learning objectives. The teaching interview is best suited for exploring attitudes, experiences, and opinions.

Next, select the expert to be interviewed. In many cases, faculty members or colleagues on your campus will make excellent experts—the best available resource may be in the next office down the hall. Also look at other colleges or universities, local communities, and nearby businesses or nonprofit organizations.

When selecting a prospective expert, find out all relevant information about the person and make sure he or she can discuss views candidly and clearly. Students usually accept the expert's testimony at face value, saving you the time required to substantiate the expert's credentials. Now evaluate the expert's ability to contribute to the overall learning experience. Remember, the purpose for conducting a teaching interview is to examine the expert's reasoning process and the rationale used for arriving at conclusions. The teaching interview should also be used to probe the **"why's"** and **"how's"** of the expert's thinking process. The teaching interview lesson explores **"the importance of . . . ,"** **"the reasons for . . . ,"** and **"the value of . . ."** particular events or actions rather than the events or actions themselves.

The expert's particular insights should add real value. If the expert's personality or style doesn't seem like a good fit for your class, find someone else.

Before the interview, learn all you can about the subject. If the expert has published works or made public statements, examine them to gain insight into his or her views. Once you are confident you have a thorough grasp of the expert's opinions and viewpoints, choose ideas with the greatest value to students.

You are now ready to narrow your research to the subject of the interview itself. What specific topics will be covered? What sorts of questions will prompt the best answers? How should you react to the expert's responses?

The last step in planning is to prepare an outline of the lesson. Consider how the expert's knowledge can best be used to satisfy the overall lesson objective. Set some limits. After considering the time allotted for the lesson, the depth of topic, and the degree of student understanding desired, make choices about what to include and what to leave out. Your outline will suggest question areas. Place yourself in the position of the students and decide what they need to know. Although you don't have to write out specific questions for the interview, you should establish some general questions in your own mind.

Three major coordinating steps precede the actual teaching interview lesson. The **first step** involves an initial meeting between you and the expert. Preview the subject of the interview and discuss essential facts to be presented. (You may not want to give the expert the actual questions you will ask since you want the interview to be spontaneous). Prepare an outline with the expert; this can serve as a guide for the interview itself. Decide on any visual aids you will prepare or provide and whether they meet your own requirements and the guest's. The initial meeting will determine what subjects will or will not be covered. Be prepared to add or delete items that the expert does not feel qualified to discuss or does not wish to discuss in public. This will help eliminate any potentially embarrassing situations that might detract from an otherwise impactful and successful teaching interview.

Remember that an interview lesson is not an interrogation. No one will be badgering the expert into an admission of guilt or error, nor is the interview lesson an opportunity to make the expert appear unprofessional or unprepared. Aim for mutual respect and understanding. If you cannot arrange a face-to-face meeting, conduct the meeting by conference call. The building of a trusting working relationship begins before the interview . . . not during it.

The **second step** in coordinating the teaching lecture involves preparing students. Provide them with a short biographical sketch of the expert or a brief outline of the lesson. This will increase their interest. They'll get even more involved if you ask them to bring questions for the interview.

The **final step?** Briefly meet with the expert shortly before the actual interview presentation. This meeting gives the expert a chance to become physically adjusted to the interview situation and to see the classroom and its equipment. It also helps you to build on the rapport started in the initial meeting and gives you a chance to discuss any last-minute changes to the teaching interview outline.

Conducting the Teaching Interview

The teaching interview lesson takes some skill. It's not a series of short speeches, nor is it solely a question-and-answer period. Aim for the informal and spontaneous atmosphere of a late night TV talk show. Make sure that you and the expert have enough desk or table space and that students can see and hear you both. Stand when introducing your guest and then sit after questioning begins. If possible, arrange a "warm-up" session in private with the expert just before the interview lesson. If that's not possible, begin the interview with easy questions such as **"When did you first become interested in climate change?"** or **"What led to your interest in political science?"** Offer a smooth way to ease the expert into the main thrust of the lesson.

The introduction of the teaching interview lesson focuses attention on the subject, prepares students to listen, and presents a good idea of how the interview will proceed. Introduce the guest yourself so you can stress the pertinent qualifications, but keep the introduction simple and take care not to embarrass the guest by overstatement. Make sure you have accurate details. Inform students that you will have a question-and-answer period at some point during or following the lesson. Present a thorough overview and don't forget that this is for the students *and* the expert. The overview gives the students a road map for the lesson and serves to remind your expert of exactly what you'd like addressed. Involve the expert in the lesson as early as possible. Introduce the class to the expert if you feel it will enhance the setting. This is optional, but it often helps in channeling the expert's comments toward student needs.

The heart of the teaching interview centers on the conversation between the instructor and the expert. Serve as a stimulus to conversation by asking questions that bring out ideas in support of the lesson objective.

Consider the following guidelines:

Use Effective Leadoff Questions—Ask a preplanned leadoff question for each main point. Even with a somewhat structured lesson, be careful not to become so scripted that you stifle interesting, open conversation. It may be necessary to rein in the discussion—think ahead of time how you might tactfully interrupt the expert. Listen carefully to what is being said and be prepared to ask for further clarification, examples, details, and other support material if required, or to pursue new lines of discussion when necessary. Notes taken during the lesson will be helpful when it's time to summarize the interview.

Remember to be natural, friendly, permissive, and conversational at all times. This will show your students that you are genuinely interested in the guest and the subject.

Use Spontaneous Questions Effectively—When you ask a leadoff question or follow-up question, you never know the exact response the subject matter expert will give. Ideally, natural give-and-take discussion will develop, but the opposite may occur. The discussion could wander into an area you had not expected. Your spontaneous question can get the discussion back on track. Direct questions, which bring the class into the discussion, gauge whether students follow and understand the discussion.

Ask Clarifying Questions—Your job as instructor? Bridge the gap between the expert and the students. Interpret what the expert says, providing clarification when needed. Do this tactfully. Avoid using phrases such as **"What you're really saying is . . ."** or **"Let me clear up any confusion caused by what you've just said."** Always ask the expert to clarify points without implying poor communication. You remain at all times the best judge of students' needs and also of how well the interview is satisfying those needs. Divide your attention between looking at the expert and monitoring students for any cues that would prompt you to seek further clarification on interview points. This can be accomplished best by carefully positioning chairs to eliminate any awkwardness in directing eye contact to either the expert or the students.

Remember at all times the purpose of the interview—to help students achieve the desired learning outcomes. Ask follow-up questions if the expert's replies are vague, confusing, or incomplete.

Carefully plan follow-up questions, but be prepared to bypass them if the guest has already covered those points. Plan a sufficient number of questions to keep the interview moving along and interesting. Examples of follow-up questions include: **"What are some other examples?"** **"Under what circumstances would that apply?"** **"What is the basis for your opinion?"**

Organize Questions in a Logical Sequence—Each question should be clear and concise to the expert and the students. The expert should not have to guess what the question means, what it implies, or what kind of answer to give. If the expert seems to be having difficulty with a question, restate or rephrase it. Avoid lengthy, involved or ambiguous questions, as they rarely lead to great responses. Simple, precise, direct questions communicate best. Avoid questions with unfamiliar or technical vocabulary that might be misunderstood or distracting. Summarize a key message before going on to another main point, and curtail and redirect discussion if the expert gets off track.

Phrase Questions to Sustain the Discussion—Remember to ask questions that direct attention to ideas, elicit comments, and clarify ideas. Some questions perform these tasks better than others. The best questions require the expert to explain his or her response and promote further discussion. If your expert is reserved, make sure your questions prompt responses other than simple agreement or disagreement. Questions phrased using "how" or "why" tend to promote thought and discussion. Consider these questions to keep the conversation moving: **"What are your ideas concerning . . . ?"** **"What is your opinion of . . . ?"** **"Why do you feel . . . ?"** **"How do you view . . . ?"**

The instructor may also guide the conversation by repeating phrases the expert has already used. This often spurs the expert to expand ideas further. Certain neutral questions may also be used to obtain a more complete and clear response. Examples of neutral questions include: **"What do you have in mind?"** **"Why do you feel that way?"** **"Why**

do you think so?" Allow the expert adequate time to reflect on the question, decide on an answer, and phrase a response. Don't worry about pauses in the conversation. They give the expert a chance to gather thoughts and give a more complete response, and they provide the students with time to finish notes and reflect.

Ending the Teaching Interview

Schedule a question-and-answer session before your final summary. After the expert's last main point, give a brief interim summary, then open the question-and-answer period. Afterward, summarize the ideas presented by the expert and show how they support your conclusion and the lesson objectives.

Close the lesson by thanking the expert. Do not thank your guest until you are ready to dismiss the class. Once you say thanks, the lesson is over as far as the students and the expert are concerned.

Make notes and then evaluate your discussion.

Conducting a Post-Interview Evaluation

It's best to immediately conduct a self-evaluation and critique of the teaching interview while the experience remains fresh in your mind. If unanticipated material entered the discussion, make note of it on your lesson outline. If certain questions did not work well, rewrite or eliminate them. Perhaps you became aware of points or definitions that would have aided the discussion had they been covered or clarified in your introduction. Now is the time to make such annotations or corrections to your lesson plan.

Evaluate the lesson's effectiveness in achieving the learning objectives. Did students have the required knowledge to discuss the topic adequately? Should the reading assignment be changed? Is there some better way to get students to a certain knowledge level before the discussion? A post-interview evaluation may be subjective, but it's still valuable for improving instruction. A more formal evaluation comes when you administer a course exam to your students—exam questions provide you with objective evidence of how well the teaching interview achieved the learning objectives and point out changes needed for the lesson plan.

<u>Summary</u>

The teaching interview gives the instructor an opportunity to be more flexible and vary presentation modes while satisfying course objectives.

Instructors must be willing to relinquish much of their authority over the lesson. A key to success for this method is the instructor's flexibility in adjusting his or her teaching style to achieve the lesson objectives. This also requires give-and-take between the instructor, the expert, and the students. Instead of presenting material directly to students, the instructor must be confident in his or her ability to skillfully use questions, transitions, and interim summaries.

Some instructors prefer their lessons highly organized, tightly controlled, and instructor-centered. If you're one of those, you'll have difficulty using the interview method. Similarly, if you have trouble following the twists and turns of a discussion, keeping track of the argument, or remaining patient during a complex discussion, the teaching interview may not be right for you.

This method does not require you to know the subject matter of the interview as well as the expert. If you already have as much expertise as your guest expert, consider another method of instruction.

Success using the teaching interview depends on a good lesson plan and solid questions to guide the expert's responses. If you understand the strengths of this method and know when to use it, you will help your students achieve the desired learning outcomes.

Chapter 6

Experiential Method

There's a sharp difference between knowing and believing. Knowing happens in the head. It's about data, information, facts. Believing? That happens in the heart. Believing requires an emotional component . . . an element much harder to instruct.

Most courses simply require an instructor to pass along knowledge and experience. No matter how passionately the instructor may feel about the subject being taught, success is often measured by student performance on the final exam. After that, it's up to students to apply the knowledge they have acquired.

However, in certain courses and subjects, the instructor must go beyond simply passing along his or her knowledge. In these cases, it's the job of the instructor to stir belief and action.

As I mentioned earlier, I teach an ethics course for graduate students at Troy University. It's a foundational course—it doesn't exist simply to instruct students on the ABCs of ethics. We teach ethics because our society wants ethical behavior and decision-making imbedded into the belief systems of our potential leaders. The ethics course I teach tries to alter the very DNA of student values, to spark a reassessment of personal beliefs and encourage more ethical decisions. I'll share a personal view here. For me, the job of an ethics instructor isn't simply to give a list of do's and don'ts on ethical behavior. True success in the course comes when students walk out of the classroom with a better decision-making system. It's my job to make sure that the ethics course enhances their ability.

Adults learn best by <u>experiencing</u>, by <u>doing</u>. Most adult learners have passed the point where sermonizing or memorizing commandments has a lasting impact. So how do you reach adult learners emotionally? How do you elicit the jolt of awareness and personal evaluation that affects beliefs?

Enter the experiential teaching method.

I developed an experiential method for teaching my ethics course. A lot of work went into the Ethics Mock Trial I created as a teaching tool. The complex, realistic, role-play event engaged the entire class in a simulated appellate trial based on a real legal case. The courtroom drama required briefs, evidence, defense and plaintiff attorneys, and three judges. The twist here was that I shifted the actual case under the feet of my students. We conducted the classroom trial on <u>ethical</u> grounds, not legal. The case appealed to the Supreme Court of <u>morality</u>, not legality.

The result? Students who took this course have sent notes to me years later. One told me in a touching correspondence that when he found himself in a dilemma later in his professional life, he thought back to the experiential event of our Troy classroom. "Your course helped me make a hard decision," he said. "That ethics course helped me understand the right thing to do."

I offer this example not to pat myself on the back, though I am proud of the course and results like this. Instead, I give it to you to illustrate the power you may tap into with a well-conceived and energetic experiential instructional approach in your classroom.

Most any course at any level of education can stuff a head with facts. Experiential methods of instruction just may also give you a tool for filling the heart with beliefs.

Introduction

"Experiential exercises in the classroom? You must be kidding!"

You sometimes get this reaction from new college instructors who have never experienced the benefits of using this method. But adult learners especially enjoy the interaction and challenge of experiential exercises.

Experiential exercise is an interactive educational method in which students participate in structured activities that focus on specified learning objectives. The key ingredient? Interactivity. Students must get actively involved and not be passive listeners.

Experiential exercises have been used for years in graduate and professional programs to provide adult learners with an enjoyable, realistic, and stimulating way to learn.

Benefits of the Experiential Method

- Experiential exercises seize students' attention and increase motivation by providing a change from normal lecture methods.

- Experiential exercises help students retain information more readily.

- Experiential exercises create a safe, nonthreatening environment in which to challenge students.

- Experiential exercises let students participate in situations in an academic setting before they face them in an actual work environment. Students reluctantly take risks in the normal classroom setting, but when you involve them in an experiential activity they can take risks . . . and make mistakes . . . without feeling scholastic reputations will be threatened.

- Experiential exercises decrease passive learning by directly involving students in reaching the lesson objective.

- Experiential exercises add a valuable level of competition to the classroom where teams compete against each other in a friendly way.

Fun to use and relatively easy to administer, experiential exercises still require precautions. Stay positive and confident when conducting an experiential exercise in the classroom. Make sure you use the experiential exercise to help your students *learn*, not just have fun or kill time. They're designed to be fun, but keep learning outcomes in mind, maintaining the balance between having fun and learning. Make sure the exercise fits into the class context. If the exercise isn't relevant? Leave it out.

Everyone should gain from the experiential exercise experience. Watch out for those controlling students or those who don't fully participate. If you have a dominating student, direct participation to others in the class. If you have a student who doesn't like talking, ask him or her an easy question. In most cases, student peer pressure will take care of these situations, but you may have to intervene from time to time.

<u>Types of Experiential Exercises</u>

Experiential exercises come in almost limitless variety. They generally include role-plays, e-mail in-box exercises, simulations, and strategy games.

- **Role-Play**—In role play, students place themselves into a simulated interpersonal situation and act out various roles. You can use single role-plays, multiple role-plays, and spontaneous role-plays. All are very effective in human resource management and public communication courses.

- **E-mail In-Box Exercises**—These exercises simulate situations or decisions a manager may encounter in a profession. The exercises develop student skills in problem-solving, decision-making, delegating, planning, and scheduling.

- **Simulation Exercises**—Simulations involve rules, competition, cooperation, and payoffs. Students make various decisions and plan strategies to reach a goal or outcome. Numerous computer simulation exercises on the market today can be adapted for classroom use.

- **Strategy Games**—Organization or management exercises allow students to manipulate an organization or some part of an organization to produce desired outcomes. Students practice as manager, employee, and customer to get a feel for these roles in real life.

Planning Experiential Exercises

The first decision in experiential exercises? How and where to use the activity in the course. Is it a portion of your lesson, or is your entire class designed around the exercise? Consider a few guidelines:

- Identify the learning objectives, the time frame of the exercise, and the number of students required to participate (minimum and maximum).

- Identify all supplies and materials that are required, such as props, boards, pens, and paper.

- Lay out the process in a step-by-step sequence to help the exercise run smoothly.

- Include a debriefing section, if needed. Don't confuse debriefing with a briefing—they're not the same. In an experiential exercise, the purpose of the debriefing is to help the students reflect on the exercise experience and to increase their learning insights. Debriefing gives you an opportunity to clear up any areas of student confusion by asking questions such as: **"How do you feel about what took place?" "What happened during the exercise?" "What did you learn from this experience?" "How does this relate to the real world?"**

Selecting a Suitable Experiential Activity

If you can't find a ready-made experiential exercise to fit your need, design your own by examining current events, articles, periodicals, and your personal experience. Of course, if you construct your own exercise, you'll need to make sure it helps students achieve the desired learning outcomes. Also, can you easily replicate it? Test your exercise with other instructors and faculty members to make sure it flows well. Honest feedback will help iron out any wrinkles before you introduce the exercise to your class.

If inventing your own exercise doesn't appeal to you, find one that does. You have a number of great sources. The Darden Business School at the University of Virginia offers a centralized source of simulations and exercises. These can be ordered from a published catalog for a nominal fee. The library at your college or university may have a collection of experiential exercises used in business or other professional schools. Local community libraries and the Internet are also great resources. Remember, even if you find some activity to fit your need, you may still need to modify it.

When you evaluate an experiential exercise, consider the following:

- Identify the learning objective. If the experiential exercise isn't relevant to student learning, don't attempt it.

- Determine the proper sequence of events to make sure the exercise runs smoothly.

- Determine how to end the exercise. How do you identify the winner of the exercise? Does the exercise even have a winner, or is engagement the whole point?

- Develop questions for students. Write them down and make sure they tie in to previous lectures, reading assignments, and class discussions.

- Determine how many students (minimum and maximum) can participate in the exercise.

- Determine how much time you need for the activity.

- Decide if the activity will introduce the subject, serve as the main lesson, or serve as a capstone.

- Determine required materials.

- Decide if you need to develop your own material and props or if you need to purchase them.

- Confirm there's enough classroom space to conduct your activity. Remember that some experiential exercises require special equipment or locations.

Conducting the Experiential Exercise

The following guidelines should help your experiential exercise run smoothly:

- Introduce your experiential exercise. Be enthusiastic about it.

- During your setup, provide instructions and distribute the exercise materials.

- Outline the important rules and instructions. Keep it quick and simple, but cover all rules. Clarify the exercise as needed.

- Keep students on track.

- Use facilitation skills to ensure everyone gets an opportunity to participate. Experiential exercises can get out of hand if you're not careful. Some individuals get competitive. Others may be too intimidated to participate.

- Maintain an appropriate pace, moving smoothly from one stage of the exercise to the next.

- Be flexible. There will always be a new twist. Don't get upset when things don't go exactly as planned.

- Debrief students. Help them reflect on the exercise. Clear up any areas of confusion. Close your experiential exercise on a positive note.

Summary

Experiential exercises prove a special bonus in the classroom if you plan and prepare well. The exercise should have real-world relevance, helping students learn skills and concepts applicable to the workplace. The basic structure of the activity should be appropriate for the desired learning outcomes and student abilities. The activity should be flexible enough to be easily modified to fit time constraints, class size, and resources. All students should participate for the entire activity. Provide clear and concise instructions. Avoid unnecessary rules and trivial activities.

Your students should feel engaged in an intellectually challenging task instead of a game. Evaluation criteria should be clearly explained to students and should reward achievement of the learning objectives. The exercise should be fair and easy to conduct, so don't spend too much time preparing materials or explaining rules. You will especially enjoy watching your students learn while having fun. Experiment! Be creative! Enjoy!

Chapter 7

Asking Questions

J.R. Hipple knows the value of asking questions. A former adjunct instructor for the University of Virginia, he has taught numerous students in subjects ranging from mass communications to public relations. As a consultant in reputation management for a firm that bears his name, he has also seen the power of effective questioning in the C-suites of corporate America. In those businesses, J.R.'s students were powerful executives, as eager to learn from him as our own first-year graduate students.

Here's J.R.'s advice on the right way to ask questions . . . and on using questions to help instruct in the most positive and effective way:

The power in asking open-ended questions was first explored centuries ago in Plato's dialogues, where one of mankind's leading thinkers wrote about the unique method Socrates used to search for truth and meaning. The lessons from the Socratic method can guide us in a wide range of situations. If asked appropriately, questions improve our listening and invite participation in a non-judgmental dialogue.

The art of asking questions is a skill you can develop.

First, practice asking open-ended questions—questions that require answers beyond a simple 'yes' or 'no.' Start by committing yourself to using mostly open-ended questions for one full day. You will be surprised at how different you will sound, the insight you will gain, and how easy it is to turn this exercise into a habit.

Second, resist the urge to give immediate advice. Instructors are conditioned and trained to be responsive, can-do problem-solvers. These attributes can sometimes combine with natural enthusiasm to lead to a reputation for a high gab factor. If you find yourself always wanting to speak before a student (or an executive, in my business) has finished a question, just breathe. Inhale. Then exhale a full breath before responding with your own direct reply or question.

Third, it's okay to answer a question with a question. This technique is helpful to clarifying, and it can be invaluable to getting to the root cause of a problem or complaint. Be sure when you answer a question with a question, however, that you are truly developing greater knowledge and information to help a student . . . not simply dodging the question.

Fourth, use questions to set the course in the future. One of the most valuable open-ended questions for moving forward is captured by a five-word phrase: In What Ways Can We (IWWCW) _____? In what ways can we improve results? In what ways can our team work more closely together? In what ways can we learn more by asking better questions?

Good questions lead to good answers. Good answers lead to learning.

Introduction

Questions play a vital role in teaching. Often, they are taken for granted. Professionals like lawyers and doctors are trained how to ask questions; new college instructors aren't. This often results in ineffective or inefficient use of questions.

It doesn't have to be this way.

Why care about questions? Simple. Effective questions lead to more student learning than any other instructional technique. Considerable classroom communication comes in the form of questions—in fact, questions play a key role in *all* the teaching methods we have discussed to this point.

The Power of Questions

To understand the role questions can play in achieving your learning objectives, compare the first two levels of learning in *Bloom's Taxonomy*. At the knowledge level, the goal for students is simply to recall specific facts. The process of critical thinking begins here, with data or facts. Recall questions help guide students to the higher intellectual processes of thinking.

During a lesson, you want your students to remember factual information and to repeat what they have learned. What questions should you ask to get this result? Knowledge-level questions. We recognize them simply as *who, what, when, where,* and *which.* Students either know the answers to these questions or they don't.

Why ask knowledge-level questions? In a lecture, you may want to determine if students have been able to keep up with your explanation. In a case study presentation, you may want to determine if students have the background information necessary to analyze the case and participate in subsequent discussions. Knowledge-level questions help you know whether students recall basic principles and generalizations before you begin more in-depth instruction.

Be careful asking only knowledge-level questions. Simply because your students can parrot back what you said in class or in a reading does not necessarily mean they understand material. A steady diet of knowledge-level questions will also bore your students. If you want them engaged in more than just memory work, you'll need more intellectually challenging, stimulating questions.

The comprehension level of learning emphasizes *understanding* rather than mere recall. To get students to grasp concepts, explain similarities and differences, and infer cause-and-effect relationships, ask open-ended questions that provoke thought and that require more mental activity than simple factual recall. Questions containing the word *how* allow students to compare and contrast; *why* questions encourage students to question the causes of events or actions; *what if* questions prompt the students to predict. For example, **"With all the emphasis put on diversity on college campuses, why do incidents of sexual harassment continue to be such a problem?"** Students must think more deeply to answer this question than a simple who/what/when query.

Good instructors bring students beyond the comprehension level to a position where they can use learning to solve problems.

The Purpose of Questions

Questions serve many purposes. A good question posed by the college instructor can capture students' attention and stimulate thinking. Questions help instructors gauge the effectiveness of their teaching. Among the most important purposes of questioning is to develop the subject of a lesson. For example, in a guided discussion or case study, the subject would be developed through questions that foster student participation. In a teaching interview, development would occur through questions directed to the guest expert.

Regardless of the method, if you plan to get student participation, plan a leadoff question. It will stimulate thinking. Phrase it so students focus on your main point. A guided discussion on the topic of time management might have as a main point, **"Effective management begins with proper time management."** You might initiate the discussion with a leadoff question such as, **"Why do we all need to manage our time properly?"**

Your follow-up questions then guide the lesson progression, supplying ideas and promoting reasoning. In your discussion on time management, here's an appropriate follow-up question: **"How do we mismanage our time?"** This question provides a new idea (time mismanagement), and now students must consider it and how it relates to your main point.

If you see a student sidetracked, ask a spontaneous question to refocus that person. Spontaneous questions effectively help instructors control lesson content, ensuring pertinent responses and giving students a chance to clarify concepts. In a teaching interview, if the guest gives an unclear response, a prompting question can save the day. Ask **"Would you restate your answer in another way?"** or **"What else can you add?"** or **"Are there other reasons?"**

Spontaneous questions also probe student understanding. If statements or responses appear to be shallow, lack focus, or merely parrot information from a text or lecture, the right questions can get to the heart of what has truly been learned.

Effective Questioning Techniques

Asking questions effectively is a challenge—even the right type of question can be asked carelessly. Effective questioning may include:

Overhead Questions—An overhead question is directed to an entire group rather than a specific individual. Overhead questions stimulate thinking and elicit participation. These questions keep the class alert, motivating students to stay engaged. Overhead questions prove effective at several points in a lesson. **"Have you ever wondered why . . . ?"** can be a stimulating way to begin a lecture. **"What could James Jones, as the company's Chief Financial Officer, have done to prevent . . . ?"** can motivate students by putting them mentally into a specific situation. So can **"What do you think the board of directors' recommendation might have been?"**

Overhead questions can be useful at the end of a lesson too. Begin a lesson summary with something like **"Well, what have we learned about board of directors' responsibilities today?"** or **"What have we learned so far?"** To leave students thinking, ask, **"If you faced the same situation as James Jones, do you see where this approach would have worked?"** An effective question to provoke post-class reflection and discussion? Try **"What will you do the next time an ethics violation is reported in your organization?"** or **"Based on what we have observed today, what would you recommend to the new CEO?"**

Direct Questions—A direct question elicits a particular student's involvement or opinion. For example, **"James, you have been teaching for several years. How have you handled diversity and individual differences in your classroom?"**

Direct questions may take reverse or relay forms. Let's say a student asks a question. You may prefer not to answer because you want students to continue to think and discuss. A reverse question directs the question back to the student who asked it. Here's an example. Student: **"I really can't see your point. Why is it necessary to have leaders who are cool under fire and effective communicators in a crisis situation?"** Your reverse question: **"Think about it for a minute, Miss Adams.**

Why do you think it would be necessary to have a leader who will make the right decisions or communicate that the company is taking the appropriate actions in a rapid stock decline?"

In a relay question, Student A asks the instructor a question. The instructor passes it on to Student B . . . keeping the discussion among students. Here's an example. Student Jim Green asks: **"But how does a crisis leader respond in this age of technology and instant global communication?"** You reply: **"Your question is one we ought to consider. Tammy, how would a leader respond to a crisis in today's age of instant worldwide information?"**

Leadoff Questions—Effective leadoff questions always allow enough time for students to respond. You might indicate to students that you do not want an immediate answer, saying something like, **"I want you to think about this for a minute before answering."** You give students a chance to reflect, then respond to the question.

Clear and Concise Questions—Have you ever sat in a class, heard a college instructor ask a question, then thought . . . "Huh?" Wording your questions well avoids confusion. Students get frustrated if they feel that they are wasting their energy and time trying to answer vague, meaningless questions.

Ineffective Questioning Techniques

Avoid questions that do not promote new thinking and discussion. Carefully plan questions so they're not too simple or too complex. Dead-end questions, foggy questions, multi-part questions, catch questions, loaded questions, rapid-fire questions, and instructor-answered questions all pose more problems than benefits.

Dead-End Questions—A dead-end question requires no more than a yes or no response. If you asked students, **"Is President Obama an effective political leader?"** as a leadoff question, a yes or no simply ends the conversation. Asked another way—**"How is President Obama an effective political leader?"**—you promote discussion. When you have to ask a yes-or-no question, follow it up with **"how?"** or **"why?"** Spur students to explain their answers and bring up new ideas to discuss.

Foggy Questions—Avoid unclear or nebulous questions . . . especially if you haven't yet thought about the desired answer. A foggy question like **"What happened in New York in 2001?"** is ambiguous—it's almost impossible for students to understand what the instructor wants to know. **"How does the role of a manager differ from the role of a leader?"** is another foggy question. It's vague. Students want a focus.

Multi-Part Questions—Avoid posing several questions at once. For example, **"What are some of the federal laws passed by Congress and the Supreme Court that support civil rights, and what have they accomplished, if anything?"** This question has four parts. Which should be answered first? Which is most important? Questions like this will result in a class full of students with puzzled looks on their faces.

Catch Questions—Catch questions give students the answer in the question itself. Here's an example: **"Now, this is the most important stage of the trial, isn't it?"** If the question implies the expected answer, how can students reach their own conclusions? Catch questions elicit little more than "yes" or "no" answers, or nods of the head, and very little discussion—or learning.

Loaded Questions—Avoid loaded questions. They reflect the bias of the instructor. **"Have you quit pressuring your subordinates?"** is a loaded question. No matter the answer, it implies improper behavior.

Rapid-Fire Questions—Rapid-fire questions elicit short responses, if any, and limit discussion. Always try to allow time for students to think and respond. Waiting for an answer may be the most difficult task for new instructors. Moments of silence can be unnerving, but remember that patience will pay dividends.

Instructor-Answered Questions—New instructors sometimes feel tempted to provide their own answers. Try to avoid this annoying habit. It only increases the amount of "instructor talk time" and minimizes student participation time. If you answer your own questions, why will students prepare for class? Engagement is education, so allow more than one student response per question, and don't rush students when they respond. Pressure inhibits students and tends to stifle discussion. Students with ample time and opportunity to explain themselves will surprise you with their insights.

Encouraging Student Participation

A final technique for effective questioning touches on your presence in the classroom and your acceptance of students. If you have little discussion, it may be that students feel you're not showing concern for them. We've touched on several ways to foster engagement (don't let one student dominate conversation, encourage all students to participate, etc.). If you make it a practice to call on non-volunteers, every class member understands that there's a responsibility to participate.

For more on how to encourage student participation, see *Creating an Inclusive Classroom Environment* in Chapter 2.

Summary

Questioning is an important way to help students achieve desired learning outcomes. You can reach a specific level of learning by designing questions to elicit responses that will achieve lesson objectives. Learning at the comprehension level and beyond will require more than responses to *who, what, where, which,* and *when* questions.

Leadoff questions should initiate discussion. Follow-up and spontaneous questions guide and support the discussion. Overhead questions engage the entire group, and direct questions target specific students. Carefully plan questions to motivate students, get them involved, and keep discussion going. Include everyone—it's your best opportunity to help all students reach the objective. Be considerate of the individuals in the group and focus on carefully wording your questions to promote robust discussion.

Use questions to help develop the main points of a lesson. If you clearly determine the objectives of the lesson in advance, you will find it much easier to handle questions and keep the discussion moving in the right direction.

Chapter 8

Providing Feedback

The comic strip <u>Dilbert</u>, created by American cartoonist Scott Adams, often sticks needles of humor into inflated institutional views and bureaucratic evils. In goes the needle. Pop goes the evil.

I relish this quote from one of the <u>Dilbert</u> strips: "Feedback is a business term which refers to the joy of criticizing other people's work. This is one of the few genuine pleasures of the job, and you should milk it for all it's worth."

That's funny. There's also a kernel of truth.

But there's also a kind of feedback that has real gold in it, real value. Each of us who has ever heard positive constructive criticism from a trusted voice knows the value of feedback in creating self-awareness, in leading to self-improvement. Feedback may have come from a friend or mentor or colleague. It may have inspired; it may have stung. Whatever, feedback has without question been an agent of change for most of us, personally and professionally.

As instructors, our tools for truing up the ideas, expectations, and achievements of our students are not limitless. We often need the skills of a surgeon to hone in on the best single piece of advice that we can offer a learner. The ability to deliver feedback ranks as one of the great educational tools for any instructor.

Feedback requires all five senses, and sometimes a gut feeling that lies even beyond those—a hunch or an intuition can often lead to perfect feedback to a student. Mostly, I've found that <u>caring</u> is an absolute necessity for delivering appropriate feedback. And a sense of humor helps.

Thank you, Dilbert.

<u>Introduction</u>

Adult learners need candid, timely, and frequent feedback that reinforces learning and improves performance. Students need the opportunity to try what has been taught. Too often, instruction is limited to the delivery of information, depriving students of the time and opportunity to practice what has been taught, to receive feedback on their performance, and to incorporate improvement as they move on to new material.

Feedback in the workplace is common. It's often overlooked in academic settings. In many traditional courses, instructors limit feedback to comments on exams. This comes too late, well after students have been evaluated on their course work. Impact on learning may not show up until another course or in some follow-up learning activity. The most effective feedback provides information that students can use to improve themselves *throughout* the course. This not only helps guide students while they can still take corrective action, it also informs the instructor when change is needed in the teaching approach.

The best acceptable evidence that successful teaching has taken place comes in the form of a change in student behavior. As important as good texts, lectures, and audiovisual materials are, they represent only parts of the process. Candid, timely, and frequent feedback to students matters more. To provide good feedback, you must plan opportunities for observing student work. That's why a well-designed course includes student peer feedback and self-evaluation.

The Power of Feedback

Feedback is information students receive about performance from instructors, peers, or themselves that helps them improve performance and achieve learning objectives. Feedback corrects student errors. It encourages students to try harder. The combination of information and motivation makes feedback powerful. Feedback does not need to be negative to be effective—in fact, positive feedback is generally more effective in changing behavior. But while a simple pat on the back or a word of encouragement might motivate a student, it doesn't point out errors in that student's performance. Without this component of feedback, the student misses an opportunity to move forward.

Be careful when giving feedback to students. Some may appear to tolerate criticism but actually perceive your critique as threatening. Defensive behavior on the part of the student may result in a lack of improvement.

That doesn't mean you should only "accentuate the positive" and ignore the negative. But only giving students feedback when they are successful may eventually *lower* achievement and motivation.

Bottom line? Criticism may hurt, but praise may not always help.

What's the best way to reconcile this near-paradox? Simple—remember that students receive positive information more readily than negative. While you sometimes must communicate areas of student performance that need improvement, emphasizing the positive should enhance student reception or acceptance. Hopefully, you'll make it easier to apply the feedback in the future.

The Purpose of Feedback

Instructors give feedback to improve student performance. In its most effective form, feedback provides constructive advice, direction, and guidance so students can improve their efforts and raise their performance levels. Feedback involves setting expectations. An instructor reviews course standards with students and provides feedback on student performance in relation to those standards. The instructor plays a key role in helping students understand the purpose and role of criticism in the learning process. Absent this understanding, students may reject what they're told and make little or no effort to improve.

The instructor should take every opportunity to use feedback—both as a giver and receiver—to clarify, emphasize, or reinforce instruction. For example, if several students falter when they reach the same step in a course, student feedback may indicate a missing need. The instructor may improve the course by repeating an explanation or by giving special emphasis to the step in later courses.

Characteristics of Effective Feedback

Objectivity—Feedback should focus on student performance and should not reflect personal opinions, likes, dislikes, or biases. If a student makes a speech and expresses views that conflict with your personal beliefs as an instructor, just give feedback on the merits of the speech, not on the student's views.

Be honest and objective, and base your comments on actual performance. Avoid a common barrier to objectivity, the "error of halo."

New college instructors sometimes permit favorable or unfavorable impressions of students to influence their judgment. Sympathy or over-identification with a student can build a barrier to objectivity. Also, a conflict of personalities can unwittingly color a judgment.

Feedback will be perceived as more objective if you accompany your comments with numerical scores of ratings, especially when students clearly understand the scales or numbers. Written or verbal comments have a higher chance of bias than scores or ratings. Feedback may be counterproductive if comments are too specific or too vague.

Credibility—To learn best, students must believe you are credible and have confidence in your qualifications, teaching ability, sincerity, competence, and authority. Try to establish rapport and mutual respect with students before you give feedback. Keep in mind that your expertise, rank, authority, position, manner, attitude, and knowledge cannot be the only basis for a positive and trusting relationship.

Constructive Intent—Feedback must help improve performance. Praise for the sake of praise adds no value except to motivate or improve self-confidence.

Remember that some students particularly need recognition, confidence boosters, or approval from others. Don't publicly ridicule students or make jokes at their expense. Offer comments in private, in most cases. Sometimes the situation rules out any feedback at all. Feedback to a student impaired by a physical defect the student cannot change would not be necessary or helpful. Be candid and honest, but also respect students' individual differences.

Sincerity—Do you sincerely care about your students? All goes better when you do. Avoid mechanical, predetermined techniques and preconceived opinions regarding content, subject matter, and student capability. At times, it may be necessary to take student effort or external conditions into consideration. You must be honest enough to evaluate each student's performance on its own merits.

Be sensitive to student reaction. If a student does not respond to a given comment, don't persist. Your feedback will likely fall on deaf ears. On the other hand, if you find a certain comment motivates a student, use that opportunity to offer a more detailed analysis of the performance . . . and suggestions for improvement.

Vary methods of providing feedback. Following a group or team project, you may choose to begin with your own comments, continue with a group critique, and finally ask students for feedback on their own performances. You'll cope best using different approaches in different situations, adapting the tone, technique, and content of your comments to the occasion and student. New college instructors sometimes feel overwhelmed with the technical aspects of providing feedback, fretting over what to say, what to omit, what to stress, and what to minimize. Feedback proves most effective when you consider the specific situation, student ability, and subject matter when determining your approach. Don't be too rigid. You'll come across as a robot with no feelings.

Style—Student feedback has greater impact when you have a clear and consistent communication style. Almost any communication style works if it is logical and understandable to the student. In certain instances, feedback can begin at the point of the student's failure and work backward through steps leading to it. A successful performance can be analyzed in a similar fashion. Sometimes a weak area is so glaring (or strength so obvious) that it overshadows the rest of the activity. That can serve as the focal point for a feedback session. The Adult Learner Feedback Model presented in Figure 3 outlines a framework for effectively giving and receiving feedback.

Here's how this model works. Begin with describing, as precisely as you can, your observations of a student performance. Did the student do well? Recognize and encourage performance to help reinforce it.

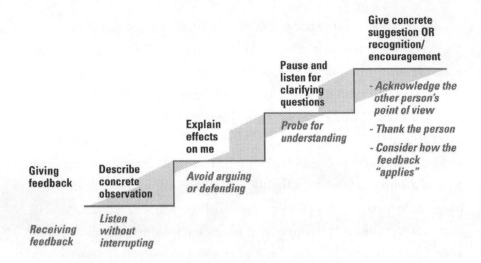

Adult Learner Feedback Model

Focusing on an area that needs improvement? Offer concrete suggestions about what actions would be more effective. When you observe students doing things well, tell them so, and be specific. When you observe them doing things poorly, tell them specifically, and offer suggestions for improvement.

The model also illustrates that receiving feedback effectively is just as important as giving it. College instructors open to receiving criticism get more—and higher quality—feedback from students. You learn, adapt, and improve your teaching effectiveness.

How to receive feedback is one of the most important behaviors that college instructors can model for students. You receive feedback effectively when you listen without interrupting and when you ask clarifying questions. It is essential that you refrain from arguing, trying to explain yourself, or defending your points of view. Those responses will discourage students from approaching you. Why? You signal you are not open to their messages. Instead, ask clarifying questions and acknowledge their points of view.

Even if you disagree with the students, acknowledge that you understand their perspectives, and thank them. Accept what they've said. Decide what to do with their input later.

Candor—Candid feedback does not need to take a lot of time, and does not have to cover every detail of a student's performance. Decide whether you achieve the best results by discussing a few major points or a number of minor points. In either case, be honest, constructive, and timely, and base your comments on areas that need improvement.

Candid feedback should include specific observations. A comment like, **"Your second presentation wasn't as good as the third presentation"** offers little value to the student. Why, exactly, was the second presentation inferior? Have clear, supportable suggestions in mind. Express them firmly and authoritatively, in easily understood terms. Specific examples followed by practical suggestions mean more than vague generalities—students cannot act upon recommendations unless they understand them. At the end of a feedback session, students should have no doubts concerning what they did well, what they did poorly, and, most importantly, how they can improve.

<u>Types of Feedback</u>

Providing feedback to students on their performances is the instructor's responsibility and should not be delegated.

You can add interest and variety to this process by drawing on the talents, ideas, and opinions of others. Here are some ideas:

Instructor Feedback—Always provide feedback to students when the need arises, and keep your comments focused on how to improve student behavior.

Peer Student Feedback—You may want to involve students in the feedback session; they'll learn as they help teach. Many graduate and professional schools use graduate assistants to help with feedback, and this direct involvement with students can be extremely valuable. More experienced students can give more effective student-centered feedback.

Have students provide feedback to one another during the class. Why? Other students may avoid identical mistakes as they perform an exercise or explore new experiences. Allowing students to work as a group means more aspects of a subject can be covered.

Students can give feedback to each other in many ways, but their comments should not supersede yours as the instructor. Sometimes it's appropriate for a student to lead the discussion in a group feedback session, but the instructor always sets the ground rules. Efficiency may be limited by the inexperience of participants, but you'll nearly always find a high level of student interest, participation, and learning. In student-led feedback, the instructor invites members of the class to comment on student activity, or singles out one student to do the full presentation.

Another technique is to divide the class into small groups and assign each group a specific area for feedback. Using basic criteria and guidelines issued by the instructor, these groups may then present findings to the class. The combined reports provide comprehensive analysis on individual and class performance. Remember, whatever the method, the instructor remains responsible for the overall quality and completeness of the feedback. If students participate, the instructor must make allowances for inexperience. Leave time at the end of sessions to cover areas that may have been omitted or not given sufficient emphasis.

Written Feedback—Write down your notes. You devote more time and thought to preparation than with using only verbal feedback. What's lost in spontaneity is recaptured in more complete, carefully considered comments. Written feedback also gives students a permanent record for reference. Rating scales provide a certain amount of standardization and consistency, which students appreciate.

Self-Evaluation—A key goal of education is to give students enough confidence to be self-critical. When appropriate, allow them to evaluate their own performances. Freshmen writing students, for instance, often spot elementary errors in their own work if they participate in a supervised proofreading exercise. Use a video recorder to tape students so they can see their performances on TV. (It's an especially effective way to provide feedback on public speaking.) Another idea? Give students a checklist or a scale of some sort to aid in self-evaluation. If students evaluate their own work, the instructor should follow up to make sure the feedback is complete and accurate.

Summary

By the nature of the job, college instructors are evaluators. *You must be able to give feedback in the classroom.* Consider feedback part of the learning process, not simply the grading process. Feedback aims to improve future performance of students and to reinforce learning. Effective feedback stresses student strengths while suggesting areas for improvement. Feedback should be acceptable, constructive, flexible, organized, and comprehensive. Classroom feedback is effective—it's timely and it gives students a chance to learn from each other. Student participation should be carefully supervised, and instructors should reserve time for their own feedback as a final word.

As you gain more experience with providing feedback to students, you will become increasingly aware of student differences in the discussion. Instructors should ensure that they respect student differences during criticism. Sarcasm and ridicule have no place in the classroom. Encourage students to learn to accept valid criticisms of their ideas without being defensive. Be a role model and show that you, too, are open to feedback on your teaching style, thoughts, and ideas.

Once you master fundamentals of valuing student differences, give serious attention to learning ways to develop helping and trusting relationships. This leads ultimately to student growth and development.

Also recognize that students occasionally need assistance beyond the scope of feedback in the classroom. Instructors should know resources and sources of assistance on campus. Refer students to other resources when necessary.

Chapter 9

Mastering the Virtual Classroom

It's true what they say about first impressions. You only get one chance to make one.

Today, though, you have more ways than ever to make a first impression.

Have you had the opportunity yet to make a first impression by a webcast? How about through interactive video? A podcast?

The emergence of technology in instruction is, of course, changing us all—student, teacher, even the instructional setting itself. It's happening everywhere around us. A business instructor in the Ivy League can give a series of leadership lectures to a corporate gathering in Palm Springs. A soldier in Iraq who wants to be an architect can ask probing questions of an online instructor in California or London.

Virtual learning is the fast train of modern classroom instruction. Make that the high-speed rail. My advice is to embrace it . . . or be left behind.

I feel justified by study after study in my view that virtual learning will increasingly be used—and useful—at every level of teaching.

Consider this quote from the Sloan Consortium Report called <u>K-12 Online Learning—A 2008 Follow-up of the Survey of U.S. School District Administrators</u>: "The data collected in this current study support that . . . it is conceivable that by 2016 online enrollments could reach between 5 and 6 million K-12 (mostly high school) students."

Those high school students will be our first-year graduate students in the blink of an eye. They'll be ready for the tools of virtual learning. Here's the question: As instructors, will we?

This chapter will help us prepare to make that good first impression as instructors, when the day surely comes, in the virtual classroom.

<u>Introduction</u>

Everything discussed so far in this book has addressed teaching in a traditional classroom setting where college instructor and students physically work in the same classroom at the same time. Virtual teaching, however, can change everything. Virtual teaching may involve teaching via a live broadcast, closed-circuit television, videotapes, or Internet-based technology. Some teaching techniques used in a traditional classroom setting may not be effective in a virtual classroom. There are very different challenges.

The virtual classroom requires trade-offs. How? The cost of two-way audio and video may be prohibitive. Or a closed-circuit television system may not be available. Since budgets and equipment availability often impact courses taught in the virtual classroom format, it is important to be flexible and have an alternate plan for presenting the lesson or course. Preparation, coordination, and flexibility—these are the keys to teaching effectively in the virtual classroom.

Preparing to Teach in the Virtual Classroom

Some new college instructors initially believe teaching online classes is easier than teaching on-site. After all, you can teach in your pajamas at 2 a.m. if you so desire! Physical conveniences notwithstanding, consider several factors before you accept an online teaching assignment.

Internet-based distance learning courses are inherently adult learner-centered, but they can only approximate—not precisely duplicate—traditional classroom teaching methods. Some things won't change for a teacher. Regardless of the mode of instruction, you must have a mastery of your specific area of study. But because teaching online requires different pedagogical strategies than teaching on-site, an instructor new to teaching online would do well to first take developmental or continuing education courses in the subject. Teaching in an online environment requires more than just uploading your lecture notes and presentations onto a Blackboard course shell. Keep in mind that various certifying agencies and accrediting associations, as well as specific colleges, require that students taking courses online demonstrate the same learning outcomes as their on-site counterparts.

Also, even the most highly qualified and experienced on-site college instructor requires training in a college or university's specific online technologies and distance-learning philosophy. You'll need several competencies, such as an applied fluency in the institution's course management system, a familiarity with tutoring programs for online students, an electronic grade book you maintain, the ability to create and post exams, and excellent time management skills. Many training and certification courses for instructors are offered —you guessed it—online. Also try to attend at least one of the technology-in-education conferences held around the country. As an example, the League for Innovation in the Community College's Conference on Information Technology and also the EduCause series of conferences provide opportunities for you to see the activities of colleagues. These conferences may give you ideas you can implement immediately.

Finally, in an ideal world, online instructors would have technical support available 24 hours a day, 7 days a week. This 24/7 technical support would assist online instructors with course delivery as well as development, revisions, and solutions to various problems that always crop up. Many colleges and universities, however, cannot afford a 24/7 help desk. This means online instructors should be able to troubleshoot technical problems for themselves, and solve various technical problems their students encounter. Technical software or hardware glitches left unresolved may contribute to a great deal of frustration for instructor and student. Students who experience difficulties due to an instructor's lack of familiarity with the nuances of the course management system face greater risk of not achieving learning outcomes. This is especially true for "at risk" students, and first-time online distance learners.

Four Generations—One Virtual Classroom

Most colleges and universities have students from four distinct generations: Traditionals, Baby Boomers, Generation Xers, and Millenials.

This wide age range presents challenges for instructors in a traditional classroom. It's even more complicated in the distance learning environment. Here, technology is the primary delivery vehicle. Millennial students have grown up with computers. They are fluent in techspeak and thoroughly conversant with YouTube, the blogosphere, texting, wikis, and social networking. On the other hand, Boomers and Traditionals can remember a time before computers. They may have to learn this new culture the same way a person has to learn a new language. An additional challenge? Many college professors speak the language of the pre-digital age.

New instructors succeed best by adapting their curriculum to students' preferred learning styles.

Using Social Media to Facilitate Learning

Several case studies on higher education document ways the digital revolution has changed students and how college instructors have responded by adapting curriculum. Instead of a strict one-way communication model—the instructor lectures and the students listen—instructors now use social media tools that allow more give and take between students and instructor. These tools also increase discussion and interaction among students. New instructors must be up-to-date on social networking sites and the benefits and pitfalls of their use in the classroom. Used carefully, social networking and media sites can be a great tool to enhance relationships with students and increase their levels of engagement.

You may recognize some of the most popular classroom management systems and social networking media: Blackboard, blogs, wikis, Facebook, LinkedIn, and Twitter.

Blackboard—Blackboard provides an electronic space for students and faculty to store reading material, videos, and audio files. They may submit written work, post to discussion boards, give quizzes, take tests, and post results to a grade book. Blackboard can be used to supplement a traditional face-to-face classroom or provide the main vehicle for a distance learning class. Instructors new to online teaching may be required by their academic institutions to take an online course covering how to deliver online education. Instructors may even be asked to get certified in online education.

Here's one example of how Blackboard may be used. For an Auburn University journalism course, students are required to research local, national, and global news from a variety of sources and post their stories. Other students review and share comments. It's basically a social network created by the journalism students. According to the instructor who teaches the course, student posting of thoughts and experiences is a great hands-on activity that can be directly related to the "real world." The social network teaches students technology skills, provides valuable marketing knowledge, and offers insight into how social media and classroom management technology work.

Blog—A case study in *The Chronicle of Higher Education* discusses how one professor at Georgia State University instructed his Public Policy class. He asked students to set up a blog the first week of the semester on a public policy topic of their choice. Students made weekly posts to their blogs addressing all aspects of public policy, from environmental planning to public personnel management. The professor asserts that his students got more from his class because they had to clarify their own thinking and challenge ideas of classmates. He considered an initial learning curve on technical aspects of using a blog as part of the course content, believing it a small hurdle to overcome if students could share course work with a large public audience. He also stressed the importance of maintaining structure so that students did not lose focus on course material.

Another helpful program is CoveritLive. This social media tool can be embedded into a blog or website, then used to comment on proceedings, link to appropriate content, or even ask questions. According to a University of Wisconsin journalism professor, CoveritLive is a great way to provide distance learning, and to offer students who may not be physically present ways to ask questions and get answers.

Wikis—Wikis came to the general public through the success of Wikipedia, originally conceived as a complement to *Nupedia,* a free online encyclopedia written by highly qualified contributors and evaluated by an elaborate peer review process.

Today, many college and university instructors use wikis in their courses. One case study in *The Chronicle of Higher Education* illustrates how a history professor at the University of Maryland required her students to post to the class wiki once a week. She used a wiki simply because it provided an escape from the repetitive classroom structure. She reported that the wiki energetically engaged her students in discussion on specific historical topics and sparked new interpretations and debates. She also read the wiki posts of students, finding that they were learning from other thought leaders in the field and discussing with fellow students information that was not covered in the regular course material. She attributed this to the fact that wikis allow easy editing and collaboration.

The University of Minnesota offers another example. The TechWiki, used by students and instructors alike, is a place to ask questions and find answers. It includes interactive tutorials on a number of subjects and provides information students need. Students can compete to find resources and be the first to post to the course wiki. Think of it as a kind of scavenger hunt that teaches students research skills.

Facebook—Facebook, the most popular social networking site, offers college instructors a valuable communication platform. Some colleges and universities set up a student orientation Facebook page to better acclimate new and prospective students to the school before arrival on campus. Instructors have used Facebook to help create connections, regardless of their office locations. A *Chronicle of Higher Education* case study shows one college with more than 170 Facebook listings, giving faculty and staff broad opportunities to enhance student relationships and reconnect with college alumni and former colleagues. In another case study, a University of Washington professor encouraged students to read and post comments to his and other students' Facebook pages. He suggested the use of social media in academia is here to stay because it gives students a method of learning that is more vibrant than lectures and taking notes.

Many college instructors want to share their research with their colleagues. To that end, Stanford University provides access to faculty and student projects on its Facebook page. Students looking for inspiration can view videos, pictures, and other previously completed projects. Gathering this information in one place also makes it easier to search for news and research going on anywhere at Stanford. Stanford even offers Facebook office hours—times when faculty members are available to answer questions on Facebook.

LinkedIn—LinkedIn is a business-oriented social networking site mainly used for professional networking. The site allows registered users to maintain contact details for people they know and trust in business—their *connections*. Users can invite anyone (a site user or not) to be a connection.

LinkedIn provides the following benefits to an instructor:

- It's a vehicle for maintaining a list of professional contacts and colleagues.

- It's an avenue to enhance existing relationships and expand networks.

- It's a source of information on potential speakers and subject matter experts. A case study in *The Chronicle of Higher Education* describes how a law professor at the University of Texas effectively used the site to start discussion groups with students, alumni, colleagues, and subject matter experts in her field.

Twitter—Through millions of transmissions of short, instant messages, Twitter delivers the best and freshest information possible. It's not so much a social network as an information network, informing people on issues or events as they're happening.

While Facebook and LinkedIn extract more value from existing relationships, Twitter generates new relationships. Several colleges and universities use Twitter to follow breaking news, provide class information, or promote student participation in school and community activities.

Twitter can be a valuable education tool. In another *Chronicle of Higher Education* case study, an Indiana University math professor used Twitter to help drive students to Blackboard, create buzz about her lectures, raise the profile of her personal blog, and create positive relationships with her college algebra students. This professor invited students to follow her on Twitter because it allowed quick and concise communication beneficial to her and students.

In another case, a political science professor at Morehouse College used Twitter to prepare for a speech. He posted a question to his followers regarding state-elected officials and social media. Immediately, he received valuable feedback from colleagues and friends that he incorporated into his lecture.

And a University of Alabama in Birmingham language arts professor tweets lesson plans, notes, and answers to questions. The professor feels Twitter provides many benefits:

- It makes it easier to keep up with what's going on.

- It helps instructors stay organized.

- It serves as a record of what has been happening in the classroom, so absent students can see what they've missed, then prepare for lessons when they return.

YouTube—The popular Web video-sharing site presents many exciting possibilities to the new professor. Educators in many fields and disciplines use YouTube to enhance course content. At the University of North Carolina at Chapel Hill, professors can put up their own YouTube channel, then create videos and provide information for students. The channel offers helpful videos for students and faculty on subjects like health and medicine, business, and information technology. The video content supplements student learning and can be used as a teaching aide in the classroom.

At Drexel University, faculty and administrators sometimes broadcast on YouTube to reach students unable to attend seminars and other events. Drexel provided a live streaming video of an environmental seminar, for example, that allowed students to watch remotely. The university adopted this technique for a seminar on public speaking. Indeed, YouTube offers numerous applications in the classroom. It's possible to watch presentations from other schools or attend lectures remotely. Additionally, students can replay seminars and lectures to find information they might have missed the first time around.

Guidelines for Academia
When Using Social Media

While the use of social media may provide students and instructors a positive forum for information sharing, networking, and social interaction, it can blur the lines between students' or instructors' personal and professional lives. Use the following guidelines to clarify your responsibilities when using social media:

Speak for Yourself—It's important to be transparent in your online postings. If commenting on the college, university, faculty, or staff, you should identify yourself as an instructor of the college or university.

Don't imply or in any way indicate that you speak on behalf of the school, only for yourself.

- If you identify yourself as a college instructor, use a disclaimer: **"The views expressed in this posting are my own, and do not necessarily reflect those of the college or university or its affiliates."**

- Do not use school trademarks or logos without permission.

Protect the Institution's Brand, Image, and Values—Whether your interaction takes place during work hours or on your own time, adhere to the highest ethical standards. You are responsible for your postings. Choose your words carefully.

- Don't make statements that insult, belittle or harass others.

- Respect boundaries between your students' personal and academic life.

- Don't initiate online friendships that might feel awkward or inappropriate to students or colleagues.

- Never voice academic concerns via social media. Use the college or university's established process for resolving concerns.

Protect Confidentiality—Through your position at the college or university, you may be exposed to confidential or sensitive information about the school, its students, or instructors. Your obligation to protect the privacy of such information continues in social media interactions.

- Follow college or university policies at all times on handling confidential, sensitive and proprietary information.

- Keep in mind that it's easy to inadvertently disclose confidential or sensitive information simply by talking about the events of your day (meetings you attend, projects you work on, etc.). Think before you speak . . . or type.

- Guard your own privacy. The more information you reveal about yourself (name, marital status, date of birth, etc.), the more vulnerable you become to identity theft.

Respect Copyrights—Online postings, like other communications, are subject to state and federal laws, including those addressing copyright protection. Instructors should follow the school's copyright compliance policy.

Use Good Judgment—Like personal use of the Internet and e-mail, limited use of social media during work hours is probably permissible so long as it doesn't interfere with job responsibilities and complies with policies and procedures. Keep in mind that the Internet has a long memory; postings can be accessed even after the user has deleted them.

Be Accountable—Use of social media that violates college or university policies, or state or federal laws, may subject you to legal action.

Final Thoughts on Using Social Media

University and college professors in many fields and disciplines use social media tools to enhance course content. The culture of academia is rapidly moving away from traditional, one-way streams of information from instructor to student and toward a more student-centered, two-way model of shared perspectives and ideas.

Some schools offer social networking advanced degrees or certification programs designed to help college instructors teach social networking like a pro. At Georgia Southern University, *Making Connections: Facebook & Beyond* teaches digital-age communication and networking skills. Through online assignments using Twitter, Facebook, and other sites, the course teaches use of social media as well as the value of communication. The instructor keeps a blog on class assignments, answers questions through her Twitter account, and requires students to start their own blogs.

Instructors who enhance the classroom experience through social media like Twitter, Facebook, LinkedIn, and Wikipedia will be ahead of the curve in this growing trend.

<u>Summary</u>

It takes an enormous amount of work to teach effectively in the virtual teaching environment. To optimize student learning outcomes, consider: 1) volunteering to undertake online teaching rather than be involuntarily assigned to the task; 2) demonstrating superior written communication skills; 3) providing feedback to students in a short time frame (24 to 48 hours); 4) devoting additional time to course preparation and delivery; 5) consulting with colleagues and other instructors who have prior experience with distance learning; and 6) making sure you understand your educational institution's course management system. Finally, you'll optimize student learning by demonstrating enthusiasm and by motivating and inspiring students during what may be a bumpy but ultimately satisfying cyberspace ride.

Social media have been incorporated into countless business courses, and they've more recently become educational tools in other classrooms. Instructors use Twitter in their classes to help encourage participation and to organize and transmit topics, discussions, and questions. New college instructors often find that large classes set in auditorium-style classrooms limit teaching options to mainly the lecture method. Social media networking sites can involve students more fully in the material. It is likely too early to gauge the overall effectiveness of using social media in the classroom. Our understanding of online culture continues to evolve.

Newer technologies will emerge. These will be used to enhance distance learning and help diverse adult learners. Through technology, it is increasingly possible to bring exciting curriculum enrichment into the classroom. Students and instructors enjoy greater opportunities for feedback, reflection, and revision. Using powerful communication tools like social media helps instructors build local and global communities and expand their personal learning and skills.

Chapter 10

Inspiring Student Confidence

One of my fellow adjunct instructors at Troy University, Sandra Kinney, shared a story that for me flatly nailed the essence of one of the most important components of good instruction: instilling self-confidence in students.

"When I was teaching 'at-risk' middle school kids," Sandra told me, "one of the things an experienced educator told me rang really true: 'If your students can't learn the way you teach, then you must teach the way they learn.'"

One of the many things a good instructor must do to help a diverse class reach a certain level of knowledge is to give the students confidence that you will do what it takes to help them reach their goals. They must be confident that you are in your profession to give them their best shot at learning a chosen subject. They must have confidence that you will bring the mountain to them, piece by piece, if the mountain is impossible to climb.

Henry Ford said it this way: "Whether you think you can or you think you can't, either way you are right."

Put another way? When students have confidence they <u>can</u> learn . . . they <u>will</u> learn.

Introduction

Adult learner self-confidence—or lack of self-confidence—closely tracks how they learn, perform, and behave. Some students have difficulty in the classroom because they do not believe they can do academic work. The "I'll never pass this test, I just know it" attitude raises the chances they will indeed fail the test. Performance depends on how intelligent students are . . . and also on how intelligent students *think* they are.

You as an instructor have the power to increase or decrease student self-confidence.

This chapter describes important facets of self-confidence, explains various forces that shape it, and identifies actions you can take to enhance adult learner confidence in academic ability.

<u>Understanding the Adult Learner</u>

The word "college" tends to evoke scenes of young students, ivy-covered buildings, dormitory life, and big-time sporting events. Is it misleading? By 2009, the "traditional" 18-to 22-year-old full-time undergraduate residing on campus represented little more than 16 percent of the college population in the United States—fewer than 3 million of more than 17 million college enrollees. The "traditional" student is actually a *minority*, strictly speaking. According to the *Chronicle of Higher Education*, 40 percent of students are enrolled part-time. A similar percentage attends two-year institutions. Fifty-eight percent are older than 21.

These "nontraditional" students tend to be working professionals who juggle jobs and family, study part-time, and work full-time or part-time. These adult learners attend community colleges, enroll in schools of continuing or professional education at public and private universities, attend for-profit postsecondary institutions, receive training in the workplace, and enroll in adult education courses at local community centers.

Working professional adult learners make up the vast majority of higher education students. The National Center for Education Statistics reports that 92 million adults—or 46 percent of the U.S. adult population—participated in some form of adult education in 2009. Almost 8 million working professional adults were enrolled part-time in college or university degree or certificate programs. The National Center for Education Statistics estimates that some 60 million working adults take work-related courses on a part-time basis at community colleges, schools of continuing education, and schools of professional education, or for-profit postsecondary institutions.

In the long term, adult learner success depends on support from college and university instructors, who must align or even redesign teaching methods to meet the unique needs of this population.

Adult Learners and Their Self-Confidence

Individuals succeed best when they maintain healthy views about themselves. Individuals succeed best at learning when they perceive their academic abilities in positive ways. Adult learners keep mental blueprints of themselves. These are composed of interrelated ideas, attitudes, and values. Past experiences, successes, failures, triumphs, and humiliations all contribute to self-esteem. Adult learners develop a stable framework of beliefs about their abilities—they have lived their adult lives in a manner consistent with that framework. We call this framework self-confidence, although the terms self-perception, self-image, and self-structure may also apply. Regardless of terminology, students act like the people they perceive themselves to be.

Influences on Adult Learners' Self-Confidence

By the time adult learners have reached college, most will have devoted nearly 20,000 hours to school and school-related activities. If previous education experience proved painful, adult learners may try to avoid difficult or challenging college courses, or they may approach these courses with little enthusiasm. Past failure in an academic subject may effectively push them away from the subject now.

As various indices accumulate, students gradually begin to generalize about their adequacy or inadequacy with regard to learning tasks. With positive experiences, they grow more likely to develop a generally positive view about school and learning. With negative experiences, they're likely to develop a negative view. Too many unsuccessful learning experiences can cause *anyone* to succumb to a negative or inadequate self-view.

Reinforcing and Increasing
Adult Learner Self-Confidence

Which comes first—a change in academic self-confidence leading to improved academic performance, or improved academic performance leading to improved academic self-confidence? Chicken or egg? Each change reinforces the other. A positive change in one facilitates a positive change in the other, and vice versa. If students begin college or university courses with low levels of self-confidence or self-regard but then experience sufficient success, we would reasonably expect their academic self-confidence to rise. Conversely, if confident students experience repeated failures, their self-confidence may sink. In the latter situation, students shift focus to other areas, usually nonacademic, to maintain self-esteem. Otherwise, they continue to lose self-confidence and self-esteem.

You can impact student self-confidence in several ways:

- Be a change agent.

- Give recognition.

- Be student-centered.

- Serve as a role model.

- Encourage cooperation.

- Teach to individuals, not groups.

- Set high but reasonable standards.

- Recognize student potential.

Being a Change Agent in a Culture of Conformity—Being a college instructor often feels like a profession for only the bravest or the craziest. College instructors generally are good people genuinely motivated by students' educational welfare. On the other hand, instructors can receive criticism as a clubby bunch of geeks set in their ways. Do things a new way? Sheer heresy.

Before you can influence the self-confidence of students, start with yourself. Conceptualize new ways of thinking and teaching. As the newest member of the faculty, be the one to initiate smart changes in your department. Your initiative, however, comes with a warning label: You may have to employ every ounce of your courage, adaptability, persuasiveness, and negotiation skills to bring changes to fruition.

Giving Recognition—When students do something worthy of recognition, instructors should always give them positive feedback. Such recognition makes students feel alive, important, and significant. Remember that you have the power to help students recognize their strengths and possibilities . . . or to remind them again and again of their weaknesses and shortcomings. Which would you personally rather hear?

Being Student-Centered in a Time of Educational Divide—According to the *Chronicle for Higher Education,* **more than** 70 percent of college students require additional pre-collegiate or remedial training to be successful in college-level work. This means you must commit yourself to being a student-centered instructor, willing to meet each student at his or her level. You may sometimes teach basic skills that should have been absorbed in K-12, such as reading, math, and English.

Basic skills also include attending class consistently and punctually, thinking critically, understanding how much time and effort is required to complete assignments, knowing services available at the institution, and understanding how to navigate bureaucracy. Some colleges and universities go so far as to require these essential academic skills be included in all course syllabi. Addressing at every level the educational needs of students is an essential part of the mission of every college and university.

Serving As a Good Role Model—As an instructor, you will be considered as a significant person in the eyes of most students. You may turn out to be the only person in your program or department who makes a particular student feel like an individual of worth and value. While all students deserve to have their educational growth and development facilitated by a competent instructor, you can't teach what you do not know well yourself. Strive to grow and develop fully personally, and you'll show students how to do likewise. Research indicates that teachers with low self-confidence tend to have students in their classrooms with lower self-confidence. Teachers with high self-confidence tend to have students with high self-confidence. Just as leaders must model appropriate behavior for followers, so must instructors be positive models for students.

Stimulating Cooperation, Not Competition—Modern society places strong emphasis on competition. This can improve performance as students strive to do their best, but competition against other students can also result in negative self-perceptions for those who happen to lose. With cooperation, everyone experiences the success of the group, and no one gets labeled a winner or loser.

Teaching to Individuals, Not Groups—In Chapter 2, we discussed valuing differences and creating inclusive learning environments. When teaching individuals versus the group, each student's performance is measured against objectives rather than against the performance of other students. As the instructor, you determine if each student achieves desired learning outcomes.

Time matters. It's one of the most important elements of teaching to the individual. Provide each student with sufficient time to achieve learning outcomes.

Adult education research suggests that only 25 percent of students achieve the desired performance standards in conventional group-based instructional methods. This same research indicates that nearly 75 percent of students reach the same performance standards when instructors teach to the *individual* level. As a bonus, the impact on student self-confidence is significant. Teaching to the individual ensures each student a chance for a successful and rewarding learning experience, increasing self-confidence.

Setting High But Reasonable Expectations—Experience shows that students perform to the expectations that instructors have for them. When instructors believe students will perform well academically, they normally do. When expectations for student performance are low, students perform poorly. Clearly, instructors have the ability to shape and reinforce the behaviors and performance they expect from students. Biased instructors, or those with a tendency to stereotype students based on preconceived profiles, set up expectations that can have a negative effect on student performance. Students grow, flourish, and develop better in a relationship with an instructor who trusts them and believes in their capabilities.

Recognizing the Potential in All Students—Adult education experts believe that most college and university students only function at 10 percent or less of their potential. For instance, scientists tell us that the human brain can store as many as 600 memories a second for 75 years and has the capacity to learn as many as 40 languages. College instructors must develop new means and different methods to tap into such amazing potential. Tearing down a student's self-confidence does exactly the opposite. So be positive and remind your students of how much they can achieve. Next time one of your students protests that he or she can't accomplish something, reply, **"Yes You Can!"**

<u>Summary</u>

Student self-confidence is an important determinant of academic achievement. Student beliefs about themselves have significant effects on how they learn and behave, especially when we look at at-risk students such as those with financial challenges, weak language skills, or limited college preparation.

Instructors must acknowledge and honor their potential to inspire student self-confidence. By giving recognition, modeling positive self-esteem, stimulating cooperation (rather than competition), teaching to the individual student versus the group, setting high but reasonable expectations, and working to release the potential that exists in each student, a college instructor can enhance a student's self-confidence and chances for success.

Appendix

Appendix 1. Selected Terms and Definitions

Achievement Motivation—The concept of motivation helps to explain why students with the same scholastic aptitude or intelligence perform at different levels in our classrooms.

Adult Learner—Working professional adult attending college full-time or part-time, likely with a responsibility to balance career, family, and education.

Affective Domain—Major area of learning that deals with acquired attitudes, values, etc.

Analysis—Level of cognitive domain in which students are able to break down complex organizational structures into component parts.

Anticipated Responses—Answers the instructors expect students to give to planned questions.

Application—Level of learning in the cognitive domain in which students are able to use learned material in new and concrete situations.

Aspiration—The hope or longing for achievement. A certain level of aspiration is needed for a student to make an effort. An example: The student may aspire to be a college graduate and be willing to devote evening hours to complete degree requirements.

Attitudes—Attitudes consist of feelings for or against people, objects, or ideas. Attitudes direct and arouse purposeful activity. Students seek activities for which they have positive attitudes. If students like mathematics, they take pleasure from activities that involve mathematics.

Behavioral Indicator—A statement of student behavior that, when accomplished correctly, indicates to the instructor that the student can perform a significant aspect of the lesson objective. Also a description of behaviors from which the instructor can draw to write test questions.

Body of the Lesson—Major section of a lesson in which learning is developed through support material and various teaching exercises to achieve instructional objectives. The body is preceded by an introduction and followed by a conclusion.

Case Study—A teaching method in which students encounter a real-life or fictional situation under the guidance of an instructor in order to achieve an instructional objective.

Characterization—Highest level of learning in the affective domain in which students integrate values or value systems into their own lifestyles or philosophies of life.

Clarification Support—The type of instructional material used in the body of a lesson to develop learning and clarify ideas. It may include definitions, examples, comparisons, statistics, or testimony from experts and trustworthy sources.

Closing—The final segment of a lesson conclusion, at which instruction appropriately ends.

Cognitive Domain—A major area of learning that deals with acquiring knowledge (as opposed to attitudinal or manual skill knowledge).

Cognitive Sample of Behavior—A statement containing a measurable, observable learning objective.

Comprehension—Level of the cognitive domain in which students begin to develop understanding and the ability to translate, interpret, and extrapolate subject matter under study.

Comprehension-Level Summary—Segment of a lesson at the comprehension level in which the instructor reviews and expands on key material and develops relationships that lead to a generalization supporting the instructional objective.

Comprehensiveness—A characteristic of evaluation that requires the stated objectives of instruction be tested or rated. The quality of a lesson overview or summary that describes a complete preview or review of all teaching points in the lesson.

Concept—A class of people, objects, events, ideas, symbols, or actions grouped together on the basis of shared critical attributes or characteristics and called by the same name.

Conclusion—A major section of a lesson that follows an introduction and body. It should contain a summary, remotivation, and closure.

Consistency—Describes the results of a reliable evaluation instrument that remain similar given similar testing conditions (similar students, knowledge base, physical testing situation, etc.) through a period of several uses.

Creativity—The imaginative recombination of known elements into something new and useful.

Course Examination—Any test that involves carefully written measurable objectives to obtain data to compare student performance levels with levels specified in the desired learning outcomes or objectives.

Course Management System (also called a Classroom or Content Management System, or CMS)—A collection of procedures used to manage work flow in a collaborative environment. These procedures can be manual or computer-based. The procedures are designed to (1) allow for a large number of people to contribute to and share stored data; (2) control access to data, based on user roles that define what information each user can view or edit; (3) aid in easy storage and retrieval of data; (4) reduce repetitive duplicate input; (5) improve the ease of report writing; or (6) improve communication between users. In a CMS, data can be defined as almost anything (documents, movies, pictures, phone numbers, scientific data, etc.). CMSs are frequently used for storing, controlling, revising, semantically enriching, and publishing documentation.

Demonstration-Performance Method—A method in which students observe and then practice a sequence of events designed to teach a procedure, technique, or operation. It combines oral explanation with the operation or handling of systems, equipment, or materials.

Demonstration Phase—A phase of the demonstration-performance teaching method during which the instructor shows students how to perform the skill to be learned.

Directive Instruction—A computer-based tutorial where information is presented, the student is asked to respond, and feedback is provided. This tutorial learning cycle is then repeated.

Domain of Learning—A broad classification of learning types. The three widely accepted domains used in this manual are the cognitive (thinking, understanding), affective (attitudes, values), and psychomotor (physical/mental skills).

Educational Objective—A statement of the student's learning goal, identifying the level of learning and subject of the lesson. Also the description of the components of a domain of learning.

Evaluation—The systematic process of measuring or observing and judging how well individuals, procedures, or programs have met educational objectives.

Evaluation Phase—A phase of the demonstration-performance teaching method in which the instructor conducts criterion-referenced testing to determine the extent to which students have mastered the instructional objectives.

Examples (in concept teaching)—People, objects, events, ideas, symbols, or actions that have all the critical attributes of a particular concept and can be correctly called by that concept name.

Explanation Phase—A phase of the demonstration-performance teaching method in which the instructor tells the students how to perform the skill to be learned.

Exploratory Instruction—Instruction characterized by an open learning environment in which the student is provided a rich, networked database of information, examples, demonstrations, and exercises from which the student can select appropriate materials for current needs and mental models.

Extrapolation—A type of learning at the comprehension level in which students develop sufficient understanding to estimate trends or predict outcomes regarding the subject matter under study. The trend estimate or prediction is based solely on the data given.

Feedback—A process characterized as a helping relationship between instructor and student directed toward improvement, change, or reinforcement of student behavior. Information students receive from an instructor about performance that will cause them to accept guidance and take corrective action to attain the goals of the course.

Follow-up Question—An instructor-initiated question designed to guide student responses to a previous question by rephrasing the original question to get the same response or by posing a new question that elicits a partial or more specific answer to the original question.

Formal Lecture—A structured and rehearsed teaching lecture with no verbal participation by students.

Formative Evaluation—An evaluation of student progress toward instructional objectives during the learning experience. Formative evaluation is not used to determine criterion—or norm-referenced assessments of student achievement.

General-to-Specific Presentation—The process or pattern of outlining a lesson's main points and sub-points. It starts with the subject of an objective to be taught and then applies this subject in specific instances that support the original objective.

Generalization—The result of identifying an example of a concept by matching its critical attributes with those of an original concept.

Guided Discussion Method—A teaching method in which students participate in an instructor-controlled, interactive process of sharing knowledge and interpreting experiences in order to achieve an instructional objective.

Hierarchy—The characteristic of a domain of learning that ranks or orders the levels of learning of which it is composed.

Incentives—Incentives can satisfy an aroused motive. Incentives such as good grades, awards, and selection as a distinguished graduate will motivate students who want to achieve.

Informal Lecture—A teaching method, often conversational. It involves considerable verbal interaction between instructor and students, in which the instructor asks and answers questions of an audience.

Instructional Media—All forms of instructional aides that give audible or visual support in a learning environment.

Instructional Systems Development—A deliberate, orderly, flexible process for planning, developing, conducting, and managing high-quality, student-centered instructional programs.

Interpretation—A type of learning at the comprehension level in which students develop and understand relationships among the various aspects of a communication and are able to perform such activities as making inferences, generalizing, and summarizing.

Introduction—Major section of a lesson designed to establish a common ground between the instructor and students, to capture and hold attention, to outline the lesson and relate it to the overall course, to point out benefits to students, and to lead students into the body of the lesson. Usually contains attention, motivation, and overview steps.

Knowledge—The lowest level of the cognitive domain. With knowledge, students have the ability to recall or recognize material in essentially the same form it was taught.

Knowledge-Level Summary—A reiteration of key points of content in a knowledge-level lesson. Designed to help students remember facts.

Leadoff Question—An instructor-initiated question at the beginning of a lesson or main point. Designed to generate discussion.

Learning—A change in student behavior resulting from experience or insight. The behavior can be overt or covert, and physical, intellectual, or attitudinal.

Learning Outcome (or Objective)—A precise description of a student-centered learning outcome for a planned program of instruction that describes the performance, conditions, and standards for assessment through criterion-referenced testing.

Lesson Plan—A teaching-learning plan that includes student-centered instructional objectives, a detailed content outline, and significant details describing the instructional elements (media, teaching method, length of period, etc.).

Level of Learning—The degree to which a student is expected to internalize a subject, values, or the ability to perform psychomotor skills.

Main Points—The primary, logical breakout of subject matter to support an instructional objective.

Mastery Learning—An approach to learning in which students progress from learning experience to learning experience based on achievement of instructional objectives prescribed in the curriculum design rather than on other factors such as age, effort, or time of year.

Measurement—The neutral act of acquiring data in the educational environment without making value judgments regarding the relative or absolute merits of those data.

Method of Instruction—A planned program of instruction with characteristics sufficiently different from other alternatives to be identified as a major vehicle for teaching subject matter.

Motivation Step—The segment of a lesson introduction in which an instructor provides specific reasons why students need to learn whatever they are about to learn.

Needs—When students have a need, they lack something a given activity or outcome can provide. The need to belong, for instance, can motivate a student to seek group acceptance.

Norm-Referenced Test—Any test designed to obtain data for rank ordering or comparing relative student performance.

Objectivity—A characteristic of evaluation that requires measurement in an educational environment be correct, factual, and free from instructor bias.

Organization—Level of learning in the affective domain in which students compare, relate, and synthesize new values into their own value systems.

Overhead Question—An instructor-initiated question to which the instructor expects an answer, directed to an entire group rather than to a specific student.

Overview—Segment of a lesson introduction in which the instructor provides a clear and concise explanation of the lesson objective, subject matter, and teaching method to be employed.

Patterns—The logical ways of organizing main or sub-points of a lesson; includes time-space, problem-solution, pro-con, cause-effect, or topical.

Performance—Part of a criterion objective describing the observable student behavior (or the product of that behavior) acceptable to the instructor as proof learning has occurred.

Performance-Supervision Phase—A phase of the demonstration-performance teaching method during which students, under the supervision of the instructor, practice the skill they are learning.

Post-Test—A test given to a student upon completion of a learning experience to measure achievement.

Pretest—A test given to students prior to entry into a learning environment to determine entry skills or knowledge. Pretesting can identify portions of the instruction the student can bypass.

Proof Support—A type of instructional material used in the body of a lesson. It provides hard data or expert testimony in support of an assertion.

Psychomotor Domain—A major area of learning that deals with acquiring the ability to perform discrete physical skills requiring dexterity, coordination, and muscular activity.

Rating Scales—An instrument on which instructors record their assessments of student performance through a process of observations, measurements, or judgments.

Receptive Instruction—Instruction characterized by a lecture or an Internet site that simply provides a student with information.

Receiving—Lowest level of learning in the affective domain, in which students become aware of and pay attention to a subject.

Relay Question—The instructor's response to a student-initiated question that the instructor redirects to another student for an answer.

Reliability—A characteristic of evaluation that requires testing instruments yield consistent results.

Remotivation Step—Segment of a lesson conclusion in which the instructor explains how students can use the information presented, then challenges them to use what they have learned.

Responding—A level of learning in the affective domain in which students act or comply with the instructor's expectations by performing an act and obtaining satisfaction from it.

Reverse Question—An instructor's response to a student-initiated question whereby the instructor redirects the question back to the student who asked it.

Rhetorical Question—An instructor-initiated overhead question directed to a group but without an expected answer.

Sample of Behavior—A statement of student behavior that, if performed correctly, indicates to the instructor that the student can perform a significant aspect of the lesson objective. A description of behaviors from which the instructor can draw to write test questions.

Self-Concept—A relatively stable framework of beliefs about ourselves that helps us act in a consistent manner.

Social Media—Web-based communication technologies that allow multiple users to interact online in a dynamic environment. Popular examples include Facebook, Twitter, LinkedIn, blogs, and wikis.

Spontaneous Question—An unplanned, instructor-initiated question used to seek clarification, probe for understanding, or control the direction of the discussion. May be either a direct or overhead question.

Standard of Performance—The qualitative and quantitative criteria against which student performance or the product of that performance will be measured to determine successful learning.

Student Learning Center—A learning environment specifically developed to foster individualized instruction. Emphasizes employment of instructional media to augment textbooks, manuals, and instructor presentations.

Summary—Segment of a lesson conclusion during which the instructor reiterates key points of lesson content (knowledge level) or reviews. Expands on key material and develops relationships that lead to generalizations (comprehension level).

Summative Evaluation—An evaluation of student achievement of instructional objectives at the end of the learning experience. Used to measure and report the student's class standing or success in achieving objectives, with the emphasis on assigning a grade.

Support—A type of instructional material used during the body of a lesson to clarify, characterize, or prove an assertion, claim, or idea.

Synthesis—Level of cognitive domain in which students are able to put parts together to form new patterns or structures.

Taxonomy of Educational Objectives—A systematic classification scheme for sorting learning outcomes into three broad categories (cognitive, affective, and psychomotor) and rank-ordering these outcomes in a developmental hierarchy from least complex to most complex.

Teaching Interview—A learning experience in which an instructor questions a visiting expert and follows a highly structured plan that leads to achieving educational objectives.

Teaching Lecture—A formal or informal presentation of information, concepts, or principles by an instructor.

Transition—Statements used by the instructor to move from the introduction of a lesson to the body, between main points, between sub-points within each main point, and from the body to the conclusion of the lesson. These statements show a logical relationship between the lesson segments.

Translation—A type of learning at the comprehension level in which students demonstrate sufficient learning to grasp the meaning of a concept, principle, or other communication.

Validity—A characteristic of evaluation that requires testing instruments to measure exactly what they were intended to measure.

Values—Students with a particular value have an orientation toward a class of goals considered important in their lives. A student who values patriotism will most likely be motivated in a lesson on the flag or the Code of Conduct.

Valuing—Level of learning in the affective domain in which students accept, prefer, or commit themselves to an object or behavior because of its perceived worth or value. To appreciate.

Working Professional Adult Learner—A non-traditional student who attends college full-time or part-time and who also has a responsibility to balance career, family and education.

Appendix 2. References

Adams, Denis. Simulation Games: An Approach to Learning. Worthington: Charles A. Jones, 1973.

Apps, Jerold. "Foundations for Effective Teaching." Effective Teaching Styles. Ed. Elizabeth Hays. San Francisco: Josey-Bass Publishers, n.d.

Argyris, Chris. "Some Limitations of the Case Model: Experience in a Management Development Program." Academy of Management Review 5 (1980): 291-298.

Banton, Lee. "Broadening the Scope of Classroom Questions." Virginia Journal of Education 71 (1977).

Baron, D. & H.W. Bernard. Evaluation Techniques for Classroom Teachers. New York: McGraw-Hill, 1958.

Bechman, Dale M. "Evaluating the Case Method." The Education Forum 36 (1972): 489-497.

Benjamin, Alfred. The Helping Interview with Case Illustrations. Boston: Houghton Mifflin, 1974.

Best Online Universities. "13 Enlightening Case Studies of Social Media in the Classroom." 11 August 2009. Best Online Universities. 10 August

2009 <http://bestonlineuniversities.com/2009/13-enlightening-case-studies-of-social-media-in-the-classroom>.

Block, James H. Theory and Practice. New York: Holt, Rinehart and Winston, 1971.

Bloom, Benjamin S. "Affective Outcomes of School Learning." Phi Delta Kappa November 1977: 193-198.

—. Handbook on Formative and Summative Evaluation of Student Learning. New York: McGraw-Hill, 1971.

—. Taxonomy of Educational Objectives: The Classification of Educational Goals. New York: Longman, 1956.

Boyatzis, Richard E. The Competent Manager: A Model for Effective Performance. New York: John Wiley & Sons, 1982.

Broadwell, Martin M. The Lecture Method of Instruction. Englewood Cliffs: Educational Technology Publications, 1978.

Brookfield, S.D. Understanding and Facilitating Adult Learning. San Francisco: Jossey-Bass Publishers, 1986.

Butler, Coit F. Instructional Systems Development for Vocational and Technical Training. Englewood Cliffs: Educational Technology Publications, 1972.

Canfield Jack & Harold Wells. 100 Ways to Enhance Self Concept in the Classroom. Englewood Cliffs: Prentice-Hall, 1976.

Caplow, T. "The Dynamics of Informational Interviewing." <u>American Journal of Sociology</u> 62 (1986): 165-171.

Charan, Ram. "Classroom Techniques in Teaching by the Case Method." <u>Academy of Management Review</u> 1 (1976): 116-123.

Cross, P. <u>Adults As Learners.</u> San Francisco: Jossey-Bass Publishers, 1981.

Davis, James R. <u>Teaching Strategies for the College Classroom.</u> Boulder: Westview Press, 1976.

Ebel, Kenneth E. <u>The Craft of Teaching.</u> San Francisco: Jossey-Bass, 1977.

Eble, Kenneth E. <u>Professors As Teachers.</u> San Francisco: Jossey-Bass, 1972.

Egan, Kieran. "How to Ask Questions That Promote High-Level Thinking." <u>Peabody Journal of Education</u> 52 (1975): 228-234.

Feagin, Joe R. "The Continuing Significance of Racism: Discrimination Against Black Students in White Colleges." <u>Journal of Black Studies</u> 22.1 (1991): 546-578.

Feagin, Joe R. & Clairece Booher Feagin. <u>Racial and Ethnic Relations.</u> Englewood Cliffs: Prentince Hall, 1993.

Ford, Leroy. <u>Using the Case Method in Teaching and Training.</u> Nashville: Broadman Press, 1969.

Fuchs, Lawrence H. <u>The American Kaleidoscope: Race, Ethnicity and the Civic Culture.</u> Hanover and London: Wesleyan University Press, 1990.

Gall, Meredith D. & Maxwell Gillett, "The Discussion Method in Classroom Teaching." <u>Theory Into Practice</u> 19 (1980): 98-103.

Gagliardi, Raul. "An Integrated Model for Teacher Training in Multicultural Contexts." Geneva: IBE-UNESCO, 1994.

Gagliardi, Raul & Paula Bernadini. "Teacher Training for Multicultural Education Towards Democracy and Sustainable Development: The Territorial Approach." Geneva: IBE-UNESCO, 1994.

Garden, Raymond L. <u>Interviewing: Strategy, Techniques and Media.</u> Homewood: Dorsey Press, 1980.

Graham, P. Tony & Paul C. Cline. "The Case Method: Basic Teaching Approach." <u>Theory Into Practice</u> 12 (1980): 112-116.

Hardy, Kenneth. "The Theoretical Myth of Sameness: A Critical Issue in Family Therapy Training and Treatment." The Hawthorn Press, 1989.

Henson, Kenneth. "Questioning As a Mode of Instruction." <u>Clearing House</u> 53 (1979): 14-16.

Henson, Kenneth T. "Teaching Methods: History and Status." <u>Theory Into Practice</u> 19 (1980): 2-5.

Horn, Robert E. & Anne Cleaves. "A Guide to Simulations/Games for Education and Training." (1980).

Hunkins, Francis P. Questioning Strategies and Techniques. Boston: Allyn & Bacon, 1972.

Kahn, Robert L. & Charles F. Cannell. Dynamics of Interviewing. New York: John Wiley and Sons, 1964.

Kolb, David. Experimental Learning. Englewood Cliffs: Prentice Hall, 1984.

Magoun, Alexander F. The Teaching of Human Relations by Case Demonstration Method. Boston: Beacon Press, 1969.

McKeachie, Wilbert J. Teaching Tips: Strategies, Research and Theory for College and University Teachers. Lexington: D.C. Health, 1994.

Page, E.B. "Teacher Comments and Student Performance: A Seventy-four Classroom Experiment in School Motivation." Journal of Educational Psychology 49 (1958): 173-181.

Paige-Pointer, Barbara & Gale Schroeder Auletta. "Restructuring the Curriculum: Barriers and Bridges." Women's Studies Quarterly 8.1 & 2 (1990): 86-94.

Pinderhughes, Elaine. "Understanding Race, Ethnicity and Power." New York: The Free Press, 1989.

Prensky, Marc. "Digital Natives, Digital Immigrants." On the Horizon 9 (2001).

Rosenthal, R. & L. Jacobson. <u>Pygmalion in the Classroom.</u> New York: Pinehart and Winston, 1968.

Romiszowski, A.J. <u>The Selection and Use of Instructional Media.</u> New York: Nichols Publishers, 1988.

Royer, J.M. <u>Cognitive Classroom Learning: Understanding Thinking and Problem Solving.</u> Orlando: Academic Press, Inc., 1986.

Sanders, Norris M. <u>Classroom Questions: What Kinds?</u> New York: Harper & Row, 1966.

Shaw, Malcom E. <u>Role Playing: A Practical Manual for Group Facilitators.</u> San Diego: University Associates, 1980.

Sheffield, Edward. <u>Teaching in Universities.</u> Montreal: McGill-Queen's Press, 1974.

Stenzel, Anne K. & Helen M. Feeney. <u>Learning by the Case Method: Practical Approaches for Community Leaders.</u> New York: Seabury Press, 1970.

Stolovitch, H. "Case Study Method." <u>Performance and Instruction</u> 29 (9) (1990): 35-37.

Tubbs, Stewart L. & Sylvia Moss. <u>Human Communication.</u> 3rd edition. New York: Random House, 1980.

Westmeyer, P. Effective Teaching in Adult and Higher Education. Springfield: Charles C. Thomas Publishers, 1988.

Williams, Robert O. "What Teaching Methods When." Theory Into Practice 19 (n.d.): 82-86.